Rusiko Bourtchouladze was formerly at Columbia University, and is now Director of Model Systems at Helicon Therapeutics Inc., as well as visiting Staff Scientist at Cold Spring Harbor Laboratory, New York. She has been involved in memory research for more than twenty years and has published numerous key papers and articles on the topic. She lives in New York City.

Memories are Made of This

The Biological Building Blocks of Memory

Rusiko Bourtchouladze

PHOENIX

A PHOENIX PAPERBACK

First published in Great Britain in 2002
by Weidenfeld & Nicolson
This paperback edition published in 2003
by Phoenix,
an imprint of Orion Books Ltd,
Orion House, 5 Upper Saint Martin's Lane,
London, WC2H 9EA

A CIP catalogue reference for this book
is available from the British Library.

ISBN 0 75381 363 7

Typeset by Selwood Systems, Midsomer Norton

Printed in Great Britain by
Clays Ltd, St Ives plc

Contents

Preface and acknowledgements

This book has been written for anyone who is curious to know how memories are made. In offering this view, I must admit we know very little. But even the little we know is a good start for those who are seeking possible explanations for how we remember and why we forget.

By no means do I hope to provide a comprehensive study of each and every aspect of the memory-making process. That would be impossible. But I do hope to illustrate how several distinct fields of scientific memory research have developed, and how the findings of each field support and influence one another. During the past few years the fastest growing and most influential trend in memory research has been the molecular genetic approach. New techniques have been brought to bear on the problem of memory mechanisms. We are beginning to develop some idea about the molecules and genes necessary for memory to be formed, and yet in many ways memory still remains as much of a mystery as it was to the ancient Greeks.

Although I cannot say for certain what sparked my interest in the neural underpinnings of memory, I do know that I became convinced that memory was what I should study at the Beritashvili Institute of Physiology, Tbilisi, Georgia. I am deeply grateful to all my colleagues in the Laboratory of

Primate Behaviour (especially to Temuri Naneishvily) for what they taught me through my first steps in memory science.

I have intellectual debts to many teachers and colleagues, but most of all to Konstantin Sudakov at the Institute of Normal Physiology in Moscow, Steven Rose at the Open University in Milton Keynes, Alcino Silva at the Cold Spring Harbor Laboratory in New York, and Eric Kandel at the Centre for Neurobiology and Behaviour at the Columbia University, New York. Each of them provided a unique and ideal environment for working and thinking, which helped shape me into the scientist I am today.

I cannot thank Philip Bradley, Konstantin Anokhin and Tim Tully enough for reading the entire manuscript and their gifts of time, knowledge, suggestions, criticism and encouragement. Many thanks are due also to those who have commented on earlier versions of separate chapters of the manuscript. These include friends and colleagues: Tony Berman, Vadim Bolshakov, Irakli Gaprindashvili, Karl Peter Giese, Matthew Nolan and Alcino Silva. I am grateful to Rachel Gordon and Svetlana Vronskaya who helped me with bibliographical searches and to Gya Bourtchouladze and Helen Ewing for help with figures. Greatest thanks to my editors, Steven Rose and Peter Tallack, both demonstrating the wisdom, perfectionism, enthusiasm and loyalty I would love to see in the editors of my next book. Ann Ashford was the expert copy editor and I am solely responsible for those errors that remain.

My heartfelt thanks go to my family for their encouragement and suggestions: to Irakli and Temuri. This is my first book and therefore it is dedicated to my parents with all my love and gratitude.

Chapter 1

Wax, Theatres and Nonsense Syllables: A Brief Overview of the History of Memory

The art of memory, with its rhetorical antecedents and its magical burgeoning, is very much an affair of imaginary places, or of real places transmitted into visual Images.
Harold Bloom

It is just another morning. The 'snoozer alarm' on my clock radio reminds me repeatedly to get up. As I start to exercise, I hear the whistle of the kettle informing me that it is time to turn off the heat. Then the toaster 'dings', telling me that the toast is ready to eat. During breakfast, I quickly scan my appointment book to see the activities scheduled for the day. Next, I open a letter and find a 'friendly reminder' from a creditor that my payment is due 'immediately'. I grasp the shopping list attached to the refrigerator by a magnetic toy and, as I am about to leave, I hear an electronic voice. My small, green toy frog, an electronic reminder to water the plants, serves its function by shouting 'Water me! Water me! Water me!...' Oh, just shut up!

We all use external memory aids to boost our internal memory system. We tend to dismiss internal memory and instead look to writing – not to mention other advances of our computer-driven industrial society – as the agent for all varieties of accurate transmission of information.[1] But it was not always so. Ancient cultures, with fewer books and without commercial electronic reminders, relied essentially on internal memory. In such early human societies, records, stories, individual life histories or community histories were oral. People's memories, their most treasured but also fragile possessions, needed to be trained and preserved. Some philosophers even held reservations about the widespread teaching of writing. They argued that writing allows a person to avoid relying on memory and therefore writing weakens the memory. It was in this context that Plato described the myth of Theuth and Thamus.

Theuth was an Egyptian god who invented calculation, numbers, geometry and script. He came to the king, Thamus, to present his various arts, most of which were well received. But when he praised letters, saying that writing was a recipe for memory and wit, and that it would make the Egyptians wiser, Thamus expressed scepticism:

> you who are the father of letters, from a paternal love of your own children have been led to attribute to them a quality which they cannot have; for this discovery of yours will create forgetfulness in the learners' souls, because they will not use their memories; they will trust to the external written characters and not remember of themselves. And so the specific which you have discovered is an aid not to memory, but to reminiscence.[2]

Similarly, written words, according to Socrates, serve only to 'remind one who knows that which the writing is concerned with'. In other words, writing weakens the mind.

Instead, the ancient philosophers recommended that the memory should be trained. The art and practice of improving and aiding memory is known as *mnemonics*, which traces its roots to ancient Greece, though the written texts of the method are not Greek but Roman.[3] In *De Oratore* the Roman statesman–philosopher and orator, Cicero, pioneered the use of memory training to assist in public speaking. He attributed the invention of the science of mnemonics to Simonides, one of the most admired lyric poets of Greece, around 477 BC.

According to Cicero, a wealthy Thessalonian nobleman, Scopas, invited Simonides to a banquet, to chant a lyric poem in honour of the host.[4] While performing it, Simonides followed the custom of poets of that time and included a long passage to glorify the twin gods Castor and Pollux. After that, Scopas told him that he would only pay half the price agreed on for the lyric and that the gods – who, after all, had shared half of the glory – could pay the balance. A little later, Simonides received a message that two young men were requesting to see him outside. He went out, but could not find anybody.

During his absence the roof of the banquet hall fell down, crushing Scopas and his guests beneath the ruins so badly that their relatives could not identify them for burial. But Simonides was able to indicate the bodies to the relatives by recalling where the guests had been sitting at the table. The mysterious visitors were Castor and Pollux, and they had thus generously rewarded Simonides by saving his life. The story has it that this incident suggested to the poet the principle of the art of memory: the *method of loci* (method of places).

This method involves remembering some real or imaginary places such as a house with arches, a series of rooms, statues and furniture, and 'placing' the things to be remembered in a sequential order within this environment. One could then recall them, for example during a speech (as Roman orators did in times before typed notes), by mentally walking through these places, visiting each location in turn. The arrangement of the places will retain the sequence of the things, 'and the images of the things will denote the things themselves, and we shall employ the localities and images respectively as a wax writing tablet and the letters written on it.'[5] The art of memory is like writing and reading, and those who know the alphabet can do both because 'the places are very much like wax tablets or papyrus, the images like the letters, the arrangement and disposition of the images like the script, and the delivery is like the reading.'[6] So if we wish to use this training to remember much material, we had better equip ourselves with a large number of places.

Two other sources of mnemonics, both in treatises on rhetoric, are the anonymous *Ad Herennium* and Quintillian's *Institutio Oratoria*. The *Ad Herennium* was a frequently used text and had tremendous prestige because it was thought to be by Cicero. It was therefore believed that Cicero himself invented the principles of artificial memory. In *Ad Herennium*, an unknown teacher of rhetoric in Rome, around 86 to 82 BC, outlined the basic strategies for effective remembering – how to choose and set up images that can last longest in the memory:

> we shall do so if we establish likeness as striking as possible … if we assign to them exceptional beauty or singular ugliness … if we dress some of them with crowns or purple cloaks, for example, so that the likeness may be more distinct to us, or we somehow disfigure them, as by introducing one stained with blood or soiled with mud … this too will ensure our remembering them readily.[7]

A subsequent advocate of the method of loci, a prominent teacher of rhetoric in Rome in the first century AD,

Quintillian, taught the method with a note of scepticism. In particular, he feared that it imposed a 'double task' on memory as the person had to remember not only the original items but also the places: 'For how can our words be expected to flow in connected speech, if we have to look back at separate symbols for each individual word?'[8]

From the eleventh century onwards, written material came increasingly into use. This, however, did not greatly alter the value placed on memory training in mediaeval education, although as Frances Yates writes in her book *The Art of Memory*, the actual material on memory training was scanty. Perhaps the most popular form of training in the art of memory was Lullism, which began in the Middle Ages and continued throughout the Renaissance. Lull's memory training was based on the names or attributes of God, on concepts such as *Bonitas*, *Magnitudo*, *Eternitas*, *Potestas*, *Sapientia*, *Voluntas*, *Virtus*, *Veritas*, *Gloria* (Goodness, Greatness, Eternity, Power, Wisdom, Will, Virtue, Truth, Glory). He designated these concepts by the letters BCDEFGHIK. These letters were set out on figures and schematizations of trees, ladders or complex wheels consisting of geometric figures such as circles, triangles and squares. The most famous is the so-called combinatory figure (reminiscent of the dartboard in a British pub). The outer circle, inscribed by letters, is stationary and within it revolve circles similarly inscribed and concentric with it. When these circles revolved, combinations of the letters B to K were read, enabling those who had learned the meanings behind these letters to exercise their memory. Three centuries later, the wheels became a key attribute of the mystical philosophy of Giordano Bruno, whose works included three volumes on memory techniques. Bruno's mnemonic was also a method of loci, but the loci he chose as memory training tools – magical images of stars, statues of

Roman gods and goddesses placed on the revolving wheels – were viewed by church authorities as being subversive. For this and other heresies, he was imprisoned for several years in Rome before being burned at the stake by the Inquisition.

While Giordano Bruno spent his last days in jail, 'memory theatres' became popular for memory training. In mnemonics, as taught during mediaeval times, 'memory theatres' were basically 'houses in the mind', and students of memory trained themselves to walk through them in imagination in a particular sequence, studying during this mental journey the images of the various memory cues placed inside. But by the time of the Renaissance, the 'memory theatre' had been turned from an imaginary symbolic plan into a real building. Giulio Camillo of Bologna created a wooden theatre that he offered to the king of France as a brilliant device for 'Ciceronian' memorizing. And all this magic for just five hundred ducats! Camillo's theatre was large enough to be entered by at least two people at once, and one of Camillo's contemporaries, Viglius Zuichemus, was invited inside this splendid invention. Viglius diligently inspected everything before he wrote to his friend Erasmus, a philosopher who opposed all mystical, inexplicable short cuts to memory:

The work is of wood, marked with many images, and full of little boxes; there are various orders and grades in it. He gives a place to each individual figure and ornament...He pretends that all things that the human mind can conceive and which we cannot see with the corporeal eye, after being collected together by diligent meditation may be expressed by certain corporeal signs in such a way that the beholder may at once perceive with his eyes everything that is otherwise hidden in the depths of the human mind. And it is because of this corporeal looking that he calls it a theatre.[9]

Unfortunately, Camillo's theatre was never fully perfected, nor did he ever manage to write the promised instruction manual explaining his memory training creation.

From the seventeenth century onwards interest in the arts of memory waned. Memory wheels and theatres were replaced by a new burst of theoretical interest in memory called *associationism*. Briefly, this term implies that memory involves making and storing associations between items. British philosophers such as Francis Bacon, John Locke, David Hume and Thomas Reid proposed that all ideas originate from sensory experiences, and that simple sensations were combined into more complex memories by association (the first mention of 'Laws' of associationism belongs to Aristotle). The various laws of association were set out. But they were discussed as a part of their philosophical discourses, and were not experimentally validated. Empirical investigation of the mechanism of association did not begin until the pioneering work of the German psychologist Hermann Ebbinghaus.

Nonsense Syllables

How do you get to Carnegie Hall? Practice, sir, practice!

It is often said that nothing is new at birth. This is certainly true of memory research. By the end of the nineteenth century a memory research embryo had been maturing and had already assumed, in all essentials, its final form. There had been psychological physiology: Johannes Müller, E. H. Weber, Hermann von Helmholtz. There had been experimental psychology: Wilhelm Wundt, Gustav Fechner and William James. With Hermann Ebbinghaus, a German philosopher and scientist, the very first *experimental* study of learning and memory was born. Historians of psychology have tried to explain how Ebbinghaus came to do what he did. They seem to have found an answer.

One day in 1875, while browsing in a second-hand book-shop in Paris, Ebbinghaus found a copy of Fechner's *Elements of Psychophysics*, a book on the 'exact science of the function-al relations...between body and mind'.[10] The importance of Fechner's work to experimental psychology caught his atten-tion at once. Ebbinghaus realized that Fechner's technique for measuring the perception of brightness or loudness in humans could be applicable to memory study as well, and on returning to Berlin he began his now-famous experiments. Although Wundt had recently established the world's first laboratory of experimental psychology at the University of Leipzig, Ebbinghaus was not invited there. He conducted his experi-ments alone, at home and on himself, without the stimulus of a university environment and without personal acquaintance with Wundt or Fechner, or younger scientists such as Georg Müller and Alfons Pilzecker, who soon became famous for their own landmark contributions to memory research. Today this would be equivalent to studying memory without grants from the Wellcome Trust or the US National Institute of Health, without the help of post-doctoral fellows or techni-cians, without computers, mazes or other endless technical supplies. I doubt that one would go far. But Ebbinghaus did.

In 1885 he published his classic monograph *Uber das Gedachtnis: Untersuchungen zur experimentellen Psycholo-gie* (Memory: a contribution to experimental psychology), which is, even today, recognized as one of the greatest contri-butions to experimental psychology.[11] What is so fascinating about it? First, this brilliantly written book of a mere 123 pages (in English translation) revolutionized the study of memory.[12] It heralded a shift in memory scholarship from methods of speculation and introspection to an experimental and theoretical approach (that is, an approach in which experiments are routinely used to test hypotheses about memory). Second, Ebbinghaus discovered and experimentally proved a number of general principles of memory formation.

Much of great science is fundamentally simple, and once accomplished and viewed in retrospect it is often so effortlessly apprehended that one is surprised that nobody had thought of it before. But it takes a genius to discover a simple solution. Ebbinghaus realized that if one tries to memorize a passage of prose or verse, it sets up unlimited chains of cross-associations that may vary considerably from person to person (for example, the word 'rose' might produce different associations for different people, such as association with a date, a birthday, a garden, a vase or a person). Such associations will interfere with the measurement of memory because one cannot be sure that any two subjects will begin on the same level of association-triggered memories. There appears to be an easy way of overcoming this obstacle: arrange the material so that its significance is the same for everybody.[13] Ebbinghaus therefore invented *nonsense syllables* – a combination of two consonants with a vowel between. One can do this more effectively in German than in English; NUH, VEG and KUR would be typical examples of the 2,300 nonsense syllables that Ebbinghaus devised for his experiment.

Ebbinghaus spent years memorizing long lists of these nonsense syllables and testing his ability to recall them at various times after the initial learning. Importantly, he standardized the experiment: each new syllable was learned in a strictly defined time (at the beat of a metronome); experiments were conducted under conditions as similar as possible; and he studied the nonsense syllables until he could reach 'complete mastery'.

To measure memory – that is, retention or recall of learned

information – he introduced the *savings score*. The use of
this score enables one to determine the loss and stabilization
of memory with time. Comparing the savings scores from
experiment to experiment, Ebbinghaus developed his famous
'curve of forgetting' (Figure 1). Memory, sad to say, appeared
to decay with striking speed: within an hour after learning,
fifty-six per cent of the information was forgotten; twenty-
four hours later, ten per cent more had evaporated; and after
thirty-one days an additional fourteen per cent had gone.
Clearly, most of the memory loss occurred within a short
time after training; once the memory had survived that
barrier it seemed much more stable. This and other studies
led to the view that memories vary in the length of their life-
spans and in the brain's ability to store them. Some memories are short-lived, can be stored in only limited amounts
and are readily disrupted; others are long-lived, can be stored
in enormous quantities and are resistant to disruption.

What are the most profitable methods of learning? What
makes memory last longer? Is it better to devote five hours
all at once to uninterrupted repetition of the task, or to break
it into ten half-hour periods separated by rest intervals?
Ebbinghaus first showed that *repetition* gives longer-lasting
memories. It is practice that makes memory perfect. 'I have
discovered that it is of some use when you lie in bed at night
and gaze into darkness to repeat in your mind the things you
have been studying. Not only does it help the understanding,
but also the memory,' noted Leonardo da Vinci. Ebbinghaus
proved this experimentally.

He demonstrated next that *spaced* training – repeated
training sessions with a rest period in between each one –
produced longer-lasting memories than did *massed* training.
Many people learn this lesson the hard way during their high-
school or college days: cramming the night before a mid-term

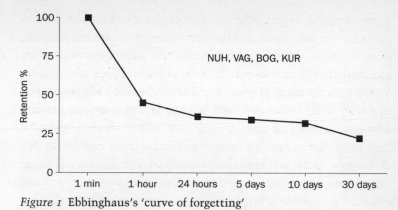

Figure 1 Ebbinghaus's 'curve of forgetting'

test might get you a pass grade the next day, but you'll probably forget the material for the final exam.

Although by modern standards Ebbinghaus's productivity was not great, the quality of his work was always of the highest standard. The key to his place in the history of psychology was his personality. He had a keen intellect and had good relationships with other scientists. He was original in thought and preferred to introduce new concepts and let others develop them. Not many scientists can claim this today.

A Momentous Quarter of a Century

If I have seen further, it is by standing on the shoulders of giants.
Isaac Newton

Ebbinghaus's work inspired a great variety of further investigations. In the subsequent quarter of a century, psychologists cultivated, polished and expanded his tests. A number of general rules were derived from new experiments. First, it was observed that early and late words on the list are remembered much better than those in the middle. These are called the *primacy* and *recency* effects, and most of us have at

some time experienced them, for example when we desperately try to recall a long shopping-list left at home. Second,
material is usually better learned when read from beginning
to end rather than when learned in parts and pieced together.
But the advantage of such 'whole learning' is not always
apparent, and it is sometimes worthwhile stopping and going
through difficult parts of the material again.

Third, the learning of pairs of items – the *paired association* test – revealed the effects of *interference* on memory.
Here, similar or different 'distracting' material is presented
either before the learning task (proactive interference) or
between learning and recall (retroactive interference).[14]
Calling your new date by your ex-partner's name is an
example of proactive interference. An instance of retroactive
interference would be trying to remember a former postcode
but having a current one come to mind instead. Other experiments indicated that memory that lasts for hours or days
becomes consolidated with time, and resistant to interference.[15] Finally, these early experiments measured the
capacity of short-term memory, and distinguished between
'short-term' and 'long-term' memory, although the first
modern usage of this terminology awaited the computer age.

More or less at the same time as Ebbinghaus was conduct-
ing his painstaking isolated research, exciting developments
were taking place in clinical neuropsychology. Theodule Ribot
in France, Sergei Korsakoff in Russia and Hughlings Jackson
in Britain published monographs describing changes in behaviour of people with brain damage, including disturbances
in memory. Korsakoff's syndrome is now one of the most
extensively studied examples of human memory disorder.

Clinical research on memory impairment is primarily
directed at elucidating its cause and possible treatment,
although there is also always a hope that an understanding of

memory deficits suffered by a patient may cast light on the mechanisms of memory. However, to uncover what cellular and molecular processes are happening inside the 'black box', scientists need to dissect the brain. In the absence of volunteers prepared to sacrifice their own brains, animal models are therefore needed.[16]

That animals learn and remember is undisputed. Pets ranging from snakes to mice to elephants were trained for fun or profit long before psychologists turned their attention to memory. Research on animal memory, however, first flourished only at the end of nineteenth century. The seeds for this came from two major conceptual sources. The first was René Descartes's philosophy, sharply advocating dissection of animal behaviour into elementary mechanistic processes. Defining animals as reflexive machines, Descartes is considered to be the founding father of objective animal psychology.[17] The second was the theory of evolution proposed by Charles Darwin, who claimed 'no fundamental difference between man and the higher mammals in their mental faculties...With respect to animals very low on the scale... their mental powers are much higher than might have been expected.'[18]

Soon after Darwin's monumental work, the first reproducible laboratory models for measuring animal learning were developed. But not in England, France or Germany. Working independently, on either side of the Atlantic, the distinguished Russian physiologist Ivan Pavlov and the American psychologist Edward Thorndike each found his own experimental way of quantifying animal behaviour. Pavlov discovered classical conditioning: this occurs when an animal learns to associate two events, one neutral (the conditioning stimulus) and the other meaningful (the unconditioned stimulus). In this way, an animal learns to respond to the neutral event even in the absence of the meaningful event. Instrumental conditioning, developed by Thorndike, is when an animal learns to make an association between a correct response and a reward, or an incorrect response and a punishment. It is a sort of 'trial and error' learning. These objective experimental methods provided the foundation for the scientific study of animal learning and memory, and developed into the school of behaviourism, launched in 1913 by an American, John B. Watson.

These were some of the early methodological break-throughs of the momentous quarter of a century in which modern memory research flourished. So in the space of two thousand years we have moved from the mnemonics of Cicero, through Ebbinghaus's home-based laboratory equipped with not much more than a metronome, pen and paper, to modern memory laboratories with budgets as high as $20 million per year. And yet we are still struggling to understand the mechanisms of memory. Modern neuroscientists may well be able to use thousands of ingenious tests and question-naires to say whether our memory is good or poor. But does this explain why? And why are memories so ordinary and obvious, yet so complex and mysterious?

Every instant we are remembering something. But how are memories formed? And why, if remembering is so ordinary, do our memories fail so often? What is happening in the brain when we remember a face, reconstruct an image of a place we have visited, or search for an answer that we think we know? Does memory storage imply the fixing of memories in partic-ular chunks of the brain tissue, or is it a dynamic, biological-ly creative process which involves many different sites in the brain? How long do different memories last? What do genes have to do with memory? And finally, what do the memories of different species have in common?

These are some of the questions that I am going to address in the following chapters. By no means is it hoped to provide a 'comprehensive' study of each and every aspect of the memory-making process. That would be impossible. But I hope to illustrate how several distinct fields of scientific memory research have developed, and how the findings of each field support and affect each other. During the past few years, the fastest-growing and most influential trend in memory research has been the molecular genetic approach. New techniques have been brought to bear on the problem of memory mechanisms. We are beginning to have an idea of some of the molecules and even genes necessary for memory to be formed, and yet in many ways memory remains as much of a mystery as it was to the ancient Greeks.

Chapter 2

How Many Memory Systems Are There?

Great is this power of memory. It is a true marvel, O my God, a profound and infinite multiplicity! *Augustine*

Consider the following incident: I was about to begin this chapter and write down the first sentence, when an unexpected telephone call came through. I talked for a while, and then turned to my computer to continue writing, only to discover that I had already forgotten the sentence I was about to write. Why did I forget the sentence that I had in mind just a few minutes before, but did not forget Pushkin's or Rustaveli's poetry, musical notes, or chess rules that I learned long ago in school? It just seems obvious that there is a difference between the fragile and short-lived nature of information just encountered (such as the exact wording of the sentence I constructed a few minutes ago) and the stable and long-lasting nature of information repeatedly encountered over long periods (such as poetry, musical notes and chess rules).

William James, one of the pioneers of modern psychology, noticed this dualistic feature of memory. He distinguished between what he called *primary* and *secondary* memory.[1] For him, *primary memory* consisted of the contents of consciousness and therefore contained information that was actively under consideration. Primary memory was temporary and fleeting: 'It comes to us as belonging to the rearward portion of the present space of time and not to the genuine past.' In contrast, secondary memory contained information that was not in conscious awareness: 'The knowledge of an event, or fact, of which we have not been thinking.' Information in secondary memory was in an inactive state but could often be brought into consciousness at will. James's description of primary and secondary memory is similar to what is traditionally called short-term memory and long-term or permanent memory.

Writing early in the fourth century BC, the great dramatist Aristophanes gives the following description of his own memory:

> Oh! As for that,
> My memory is of two sorts, long and short:
> With them who owe me ought it never fails;
> My creditors, indeed, complain of it
> As mainly apt to leak and lose its reckoning.[2]

At least as far back as the ancient Greeks, people believed that short-term memory differed fundamentally in nature from long-term memory. Nonetheless, there has been a long, continuing and often bitter debate about the need for postulating a separate system for short-term memory and one for long-term memory. But what does a memory system mean anyway? Like many other complex concepts, that of a memory system can be understood in different ways. According to one of the most popular views, a memory system is defined in terms of its brain structures, the length of time that information is stored in them, and the type of information remembered.[3] If so, how many memory systems are there?

The predominant view among memory researchers until the late 1950s was that memory is a unitary system. To make a simple analogy, in a unitary system there would be only one route between New York and Los Angeles. In the beginning this would be a small footpath but the more it was used the more it would grow until it became a multi-lane freeway. By the late 1950s and early 1960s, however, the unitary view began to fade, and the multiple system approach came to flourish. Under the same analogy, in a multiple memory system there have always been many possible ways of travelling between New York and Los Angeles. Some of these have become permanent routes, some still wait for more development, and others are represented by faint footprints in the desert sands continuously overblown by the action of the wind.

What happened to make most of the memory researchers abandon the unitary view of memory and embrace the multiple system approach? Interestingly, one of the most important influences came from outside the domain of traditional psychology. It was the time of rapid development in computer technology, and that led memory researchers to think about memory in new ways. As the two fields of computer science and experimental psychology developed further, it was natural to look for common organizing principles in both.

The belief that there are common foundations for both brain science and computer science has come and gone and come again. In the 1950s, the notion that neurons were digital 'on–off' switches, and that brains and newly emerging digital computers therefore had similar structural organizations, captured the imagination of scientists. It became fashionable for psychologists to adopt the terms and concepts of the information-processing approach used by computer scientists. Terms such as short-term storage buffers, long-term storage units, processing components, nodes, modules and binary units of information were quickly incorporated into the psychologists' vocabulary and used to explain human memory.

The second piece of evidence for the multiple memory system came in the late 1950s when some amazing new data appeared suggesting that short-term memory has a tiny storage capacity, relatively rapid input and retrieval, and wanes fast if rehearsal is prevented. Long-term memory, on the other hand, has huge capacity, but tends to be slower to register information and retrieve it. Finally, the strongest evidence for multiple memory systems came from studies of brain-damaged patients. It became clear that memory does not play tricks in an 'all or none' fashion – some memories might be lost, some disturbed for a while, others could remain always fresh and intact. I shall outline some of this research below, but I shall return to the multiple memory system concept later when describing more recent findings.

The Magic Number Seven

In 1887 a London teacher, Joseph Jacobs, became interested in studying the mental capacity of his pupils. Prompted by Ebbinghaus's work, he devised the technique that has become known as the *memory span procedure*.[4] Jacobs presented his subjects with a sequence of items and then asked them to repeat the sequence back verbatim. Typically, he would begin with one item, often a number, and gradually increase the length of the sequence to the point where the pupil would fail to repeat it correctly. The point at which the pupil was right fifty per cent of the time was designated as the subject's memory span.

In general, the capacity of short-term memory is pretty humble. Try to memorize the following letters in correct order (you could alternatively use digits if you want):

ARMDOGMUGSOSCIAPUBTOP

I would guess it is beyond your short-term memory capacity. But don't be disappointed. You were presented with twenty-one items, whilst normal adults can typically remember only about seven. How do we know this? In the 1950s, George Miller of Harvard University tested many people on their ability to recall, in correct order, various strings of letters, digits and words. This became the central theme of his classic paper, 'The magic number seven, plus or minus two: some limits on our capacity for processing information'.[5] Miller found that immediate memory span was governed by the number of 'chunks' rather than by the number of items, and averaged about seven 'chunks'. According to Miller, a 'chunk' is an integrated piece of information. The meaningful packaging of information into chunks for storage in short-term memory is called *chunking*. So a familiar letter combination such as MUG is likely to act as a 'chunk', while a less significant one such as VAH would probably not. Now, look again at the list and separate these twenty-one items into meaningful chunks:

ARM DOG MUG SOS CIA PUB TOP

No problem, right? Chunking allows us to remember bank-card numbers, postcodes, telephone numbers, and even the spelling of complex words such as *parallelepiped*. Kids often use chunking when they learn the alphabet – to them, ABCDEFG often sounds like a single word. Chess grand-masters and expert card players chunk when they memorize and reproduce patterns of games.

What else might help us retain a series of letters, digits or words? Typically, recall is improved by inserting a brief pause between successive groupings. This is called *rhythmic chunking*. An amazing effect of such rhythmic chunking is described by Ian

M. L. Hunter in his paper 'An exceptional talent for calculative thinking'.[6] Hunter writes how Professor Alexander Craig Aitken of Edinburgh, a mathematician with an exceptional memory, memorized the first thousand decimals of *pi*, the ratio of the circumference of a circle to its diameter. Apparently, Aitken had no problem in remembering numbers if he first put them down in rows of fifty, comprising ten groups of five, and then read them rhythmically. The key, however, was the presentation rate of the digits. The professor's performance was perfect only if the digits were presented at a rate of about five per second. But when Hunter attempted to slow down the presentation rate to one digit per second, Aitken's memory was unremarkable. Aitken himself commented that it was 'like learning to ride a bicycle slowly'. Taking his complaint into consideration, Hunter increased the rate to five per second again and Aitken's memory span was back in business. He had no problem in repeating strings of fifteen digits in any order.

But what about ordinary people who can cram into short-term memory no more than seven items? Would practice break the grip of the 'magic seven'? A perfect example of *how* practice improves memory span is given by scientists from Carnegie Mellon University at Pittsburgh. In 1980, Anders Ericsson, William Chase and Steve Faloon described the unusual memory capabilities of a young man known as S.F., an undergraduate with 'average memory abilities'.[7] In Ericsson's experiment, S.F. was read random digits and then asked to recall the sequence. If the sequence was reported correctly, the next sequence was increased by one digit; if not, it was decreased by one digit. This monotonous, boring and yet important experiment was repeated daily over twenty months. But practice is always rewarded: after more than 230 hours of exercise, S.F.'s memory span increased from seven to seventy-nine digits.

How was he able to keep so many digits in his short-term

memory store? Was the capacity of short-term storage increased by determined practice? Will practice increase our short-term memory store? Whilst practice is usually good, I would not waste my time with this particular form. Ericsson and his team concluded that nothing had happened to S.F.'s short-term memory capacity. The sizes of his 'chunks' were almost always three or four digits, and he never generated a mnemonic association for more than five digits. And disappointingly, when alphabetical letters were presented, S.F.'s memory span was trivial. So how did he manage to remember seventy-nine digits?

The trick was simple. Although not attempting to cheat, S.F. was using a long-term strategy to perform well on a short-term memory task. Here is the secret: it turned out that S.F. was an enthusiastic long-distance runner who competed in races throughout the United States. When memorizing the digits, he used his athletic knowledge to translate the digit strings into running times. For example, he memorized '3492' as '3 minutes and 49 point 2 seconds, near world-record mile time'. During the first few months of training S.F. constructed a set of mnemonic associations based initially on running times and then supplemented with dates (1944 was 'near the end of World War II') or ages (893 was '89 point 3, very old man') for those sequences that could not be categorized as recording running times.

The Distractor

In the late 1950s, John Brown in England, and Lloyd and Margaret Peterson, a married couple in the USA, independently found that if subjects were distracted from practising new information, then in a matter of seconds, the information would often be entirely forgotten. The procedure that enabled them to come to such a conclusion became known as the Brown–Peterson distractor technique.[8]

This technique is neat and easy to replicate. For example, in the Petersons' experiment, subjects were presented with a meaningless set of three letters (say, TLP) and asked to recall the letters after varying periods of delay (usually no more than eighteen seconds). This should not be a problem. However, to prevent the subjects from rehearsing the letters during the delay period they were required to do a distractor task. That is, immediately after the three letters were given, a random number, say 573, was also presented. The subjects were asked to repeat the number and then proceed to count backward from it in threes (573, 570, 567, 564 and so forth) until the experimenter gave the signal to stop. At this point the subjects were required to recall the three letters. Each subject would be given many trials with different letters and numbers. It appeared that subjects performed perfectly well for the first trial or two, but after they had been through many trials, they forgot very rapidly. Typically, after just eighteen seconds of distracting calculations, only one in every ten three-letter combinations will be correctly remembered. So ninety per cent of the information is forgotten in just a few seconds.

These results generated enormous excitement for at least two reasons. First, the Brown–Peterson procedure offered a simple and reproducible technique for studying short-term forgetting. Second, the Petersons attributed the rapid forgetting to *trace decay*. This theory assumed that if the material is not repeatedly rehearsed, a memory trace will automatically fade away over time. Memory is like perfume, it evaporates with time. In contrast, *interference* theory assumes that forgetting reflects the distraction of the memory traces by other traces. At the time of these experiments, it was widely accepted that long-term forgetting was based on the principles of interference rather than decay. So if short-term forgetting was indeed due to trace decay, then at least two different memory systems would be known. Thus, the Petersons' interpretation of short-term forgetting had a stunning effect on both the 'unitary' and 'multiple' memory-system camps – the former did not like it, whereas the latter did.

Nonetheless, a couple of years later, this interpretation was challenged by Geoffrey Keppel of the University of California, Berkeley, and Benton Underwood of the University of Nottingham in the UK, who provided convincing evidence that the short-term forgetting observed in the Brown–Peterson task was the result of the build-up of interference from consonants that had been remembered on earlier trials.[9] They found that on the first trial subjects showed virtually no forgetting of the three-letter combinations after completing the distractor task. That was explained by the absence of any similar previous items that might cause interference. But researchers claimed that after a few trials proactive interference will evolve, and people will have trouble distinguishing between letters presented earlier and those on the current trial.

In the following years a flood of experimental evidence appeared favouring either the interference theory or the trace decay explanation of short-term forgetting. As so often happens, it turned out that both camps were right to an extent – short-term forgetting involves both the weakening of the trace, and the problem of retrieving the memory or discriminating it from other competing traces.

Magic Number or Magic Spell?

Evidence for the short-term and long-term memory systems came from the demonstration that certain tasks appear to have two separable and quite different components. The most popular and extensively studied task of this kind is *free recall*. A typical experiment involves giving subjects a long list of unrelated items to study and then asking them to recall as many as possible in any order they want. Usually, the first few items and the last few items are more likely to be recalled – respectively referred to as the *primacy* and *recency* effects. Although the roots of this technique can be found as early as the beginning of the century, the method was not thoroughly explored until the mid-1960s.

Why do the middle items become inferior, less important? One simple interpretation of this result is that the first items are given sufficient rehearsal to allow them to enter long-term memory, whereas the middle items are not likely to receive as much rehearsal because they enter short-term memory when it is already jam-packed with the first items. What about the last items? It is likely that they are still in short-term store at the time of recall and that is why they can be quickly remembered. However interpreted, the existence of primacy and recency effects has been cited as strong evidence in favour of dichotomy in short-term and long-term memory systems.

The method was soon used to estimate the capacity of short-term memory. As a result, some researchers claimed that short-term storage can handle two to five items – sadly, an amount smaller than Miller's estimate of a magic seven. Others have implied that the capacity of short-term memory is better defined not in terms of items or chunks but in terms of a period of time before the trace wanes. This lasts for about 1.5 to 2 seconds. For example, psychologists Richard Schweickert of Purdue University and Brian Boruff of the University of Florida tested subjects' memory span for many different items such as digits, consonants or colour names. They summarized their observations under the intriguing title 'Short-term memory capacity: magic number or magic spell?'[10] In the paper, they argued that the memory span for these different items equalled the number of items that people can pronounce in about 1.5 seconds. Measured one way or the other, the capacity of short-term memory appears to be small.

Clinical Evidence

The idea, derived from psychological studies, that there are separate short-term and long-term memory systems soon received strong confirmation from observations of the effects of brain injury and diseases. Head damage is, perhaps, one of the leading causes of memory loss. A blow to the head may cause a momentary loss of consciousness and concussion, or it may result in a coma that can last for months and even years. Sometimes even a relatively mild head injury is sufficient to disrupt the remembrance of ongoing events or, to be precise, the process of *consolidation* – the transformation of memory from short-term memory to long-term memory.[11] Often, when this happens, a person may continue with routine activities, and only later does it become clear that he or she has absolutely no recollection of what went on earlier. This is a common occurrence in contact sports. For example, a boxer may continue fighting for several more rounds after being knocked down, and may even go on to win. But on subsequent questioning, it becomes obvious that he had no memory of what actually happened during those rounds.

More serious brain injury will cause a loss of consciousness that results in coma. A general rule of thumb is that the longer the period of coma, the greater the memory loss for the events that happened before the accident. On recovering consciousness it is usual for people not to regain all their memories at once. Rather, they seem to pass through a period of confusion and disorientation, in which they will have strange gaps in memory for daily events and recognition of people and things. For example, a person may remember a visit by a parent but not by a friend, or the name of a sister but not a brother. This stage of 'spotty' memory is also character-ized by selective loss of memory for events that occurred before the injury, and sometimes even for things that hap-pened years before. Similar consequences, known as *retro-grade amnesia*, follow anaesthetic coma, drug abuse, disruption of the blood supply to the brain, brain infections or electroconvulsive shock therapy.[12]

As the patient recovers, there is usually a steady and gradual shrinkage of retrograde amnesia, but often the retrograde amnesia is very long-lasting. The temporary blocking of rela-tively recent memory may be so marked that recollection of several years of recent life may be entirely eliminated. For a limited time patients may give the current date as being several years earlier, and believe themselves to be correspond-ingly younger, as described in one of the earliest reports by the London neuropsychologist Ritchie Russell of a Polish pilot who crashed his aeroplane in the year 1941.[13] When he recov-ered from his coma three weeks later, he was still confused and said that the year was 1936. When he was asked about the war with Germany, he replied, 'We are not ready yet.' It may sound strange, but the recovery of memory depends not so much on the relative importance of the events forgotten as on the time before the injury that the events occurred. Although memories often return in an irregular, hit-or-miss order, the older memories typically come back first. Here is another story of retrograde amnesia described by Russell.

One summer day in 1933, a twenty-two-year-old man known by the initials P.A.S. was thrown from his motorcycle after an accident. He injured the left frontal region of his brain, although he did not fracture his skull. A week after the accident he had no recollection of the five years he had spent in Australia, nor did he remember the last two years in which he had lived and worked in England. Two weeks after the injury, his Australian memories came back, but the memories of the past two years were still blank. On returning to his village three weeks later, he was disoriented and had no recollection of ever having lived or worked there before. Fortunately, his memory of the events of the past two years gradually returned, and after seven more weeks he could recall everything up to a few minutes before the accident. A brief retrograde amnesia is often an accurate indication of mental normality; and P.A.S. indeed soon returned to normal life.

Nonetheless, when all does not go as well as it did for P.A.S. the tragic consequences of accidents may produce a more devastating memory problem called *anterograde amnesia*. This term refers to a brain-damaged person's inability to consolidate and remember new things. In a person with anterograde amnesia the short-term and remote memory are still intact. However, the brain no longer transfers information properly from short-term to long-term store. When this happens, a person is stuck forever in time, as seems to be the case with N.A.[14] In 1960 this patient was a bright young man in the Air Force, living in a dormitory with a room-mate who liked to fool around with a miniature fencing foil. One day in December, N.A. turned around at the wrong time, just as his room-mate was performing a lunge with the foil. The blade entered N.A.'s right nostril and subsequently lodged in the left side of his brain. From that moment, for N.A., time stopped.

Although there remains some controversy as to the precise location and extent of damage that N.A. sustained, it is clear that parts of his brain responsible for laying down new memories are damaged beyond repair. Despite having vivid memories of repairing an old Cadillac and driving it across America two years before the accident, he has faint recollection of yesterday, or even an hour ago. He likes television, but every time there is a commercial break he loses track of whatever programme he is watching and, even without any interruptions, he can scarcely remember what he was watching a half an hour before. 'Even significant events are recalled vaguely, if at all,' writes Larry Squire, a leading neuroscientist at the University of California, San Diego. 'He knows that "Watergate" signifies some political event, but cannot provide additional information... The events of daily life present an even bigger problem. He loses track of his possessions, forgets what he has done, and forgets whom he has visited... He cannot cook for himself satisfactorily, because the correct sequence of steps places too great a burden on his memory... It is extraordinary how unremarkable amnesia can appear on first impression, yet how profound and devastating an effect it can nevertheless have.'

Many other patients have been described who have selective deficits in short-term or long-term memory. Some, like K.F. for example, had substantial difficulty holding new information for short periods of time but little problem with long-term learning.[15] But people suffering from amnesia do not have a total inability to consolidate new information and to retain it for long periods. Both the things that N.A. or K.F. – and the better-known H.M., whom we meet later – *can't* remember and the things that they *can* remember are clues to the complexities of memory. The memory deficit is *selective* and most evident when patients are required to consciously recall or recognize information presented to them after the onset of amnesia. What is more, such patients' behaviour can be altered by experience, and they can learn and remember some new information, but this becomes apparent only if the patient is tested using special memory tests, as I shall describe in Chapter 3.

Long-term Memory

Great is this power of memory, exceedingly great, O my God – a large and boundless inner hall! Who has plumbed the depths of it? *Augustine*

We have just learned that some people might have a grossly defective memory for recent events but normal long-term memory. The clinical literature certainly favours the existence of separate short-term and long-term stores. But regardless of how one feels about the distinction between short-term and long-term memory, everyone will admit to having memories of years ago. Indeed, long-term memory appears to have a virtually boundless duration and capacity.

Try to answer the following list of questions. When did you leave school? Does an elephant fly? How many grams in a kilogram? What is the capital of Germany? Who is the director of *One Flew Over the Cuckoo's Nest*? What did you have for dinner last Thursday? Some of these questions are very easy to answer, while others are not. For example, you will answer instantly the year you graduated from school, that elephants do not fly, and that there are a thousand grams in a kilogram. You might take a little time to recall that the capital of Germany is Berlin (but not Bonn any more) and that Milos Forman is the director of the Oscar-winning film *One Flew Over the Cuckoo's Nest*. But unless you had a special dinner on Thursday evening, or you are a person of exceptionally routine habits – always salmon, rice and a glass of Pinot Grigio on Thursdays – chances are that you will have only a cloudy idea of what you ate that evening.

Keeping track of all these memories is no easy task. Yet the reason we can answer hundreds of thousands of dissimilar questions rapidly and confidently is because our long-term memory is highly organized, and we possess ways to efficiently analyse, manipulate, search and retrieve memory. To fully understand the nature of long-term memory, scientists have attempted to partition and categorize long-term memory in different ways. The variety of proposed divisions of memory provoked a science writer, Rebecca Rupp, to compare it to a psychologist's version of the mythological Hydra, 'a monster that whenever you manage to chop off one head sprouts two others in its place'.[16] Indeed, more than three dozen different names have been proposed for different types of memory, all 'campaigning' for widespread usage. For simplicity, these terms are combined under the single phrase *declarative* memory, which includes memories of both facts and past episodes from our lives. This type of memory is contrasted with *non-declarative* memory, which includes memories of skills and habits, and emotional memory (Figure 2). Let's inspect them in turn.

Semantic and Episodic Memory

In this life, we want nothing but Facts, nothing but Facts!
Charles Dickens

The distinction between semantic and episodic memory has been noted by many philosophers and psychologists over the centuries on the basis of intuition and introspection. In modern times, however, it is a Canadian psychologist, Endel Tulving, who should be credited for the development and popularization of these two systems of memory.[17]

Episodic memory is the memory of particular times, places and contexts. It explicitly refers to specific events and

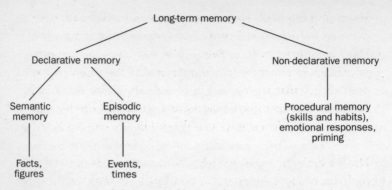

Figure 2 Functional divisions of human long-term memory

experiences in our life. Episodic memories are bound to particular autobiographical events. Recall your school or college graduation day, your first job interview, your first kiss or your wedding ceremony and you are calling upon episodic memories. Such emotional highs and lows as falling in love, witnessing a crime or watching a favourite football team scoring a winning goal in a championship game, to name a few, may have an astonishing influence on our episodic memories. In this way, you won't have much difficulty recalling what you had for dinner last Thursday if at that dinner you received your first job offer to pay you six figures. On the contrary, you will have a vivid picture of the food and wine served, the suit you were wearing, and so on.

All memories start as episodic, but only unique experiences survive as time goes by. Those that do not have freshness and characteristic flavour tend to go downhill with time. Only exceptional people are likely to remember in colourful detail their seventy-seventh swim in the Caribbean, their eighty-first kiss or their 567th working day. Sameness leads to forgetfulness, as seen through the eyes of the writer John McPhee in the novel *Silk Parachute*:

When your mother is ninety-nine years old, you have so many memories of her that they tend to overlap, intermingle, and blur. It is extremely difficult to single out one or two, impossible to remember any that exemplify the whole. It has been alleged that when I was in college, she heard that I had stayed up all night playing poker and wrote me a letter that used the word 'shame' forty-two times. I do not recall this.[18]

Unlike episodic memory, semantic memory is context-free knowledge of facts, language or concepts. Semantic memories surpass the conditions in which they were formed and stay comparatively fresh. Semantic memory stores general knowledge about the world that is not bound to specific experiences. As such, semantic memory encompasses an incredible amount of information. The definitions of words such as 'dog' and 'cat', the meanings of road signs such as 'stop' and 'H', rules such as 'Do not smoke' and concepts not tied to specific events, such as 'There are a hundred centimetres in one metre', are essential material of semantic memory.

When and how is it formed? Let me give you an example. My son Irakli was one year old when he saw a cow for the first time. At that time we were on holiday at our summer cottage in the beautiful village of Seony in the former Soviet republic of Georgia. Every morning we used to visit a local peasant, Eugenia, to buy milk. That is where Irakli met for the first time a milk-producing creature which he began to identify as a *moo*. So he learned that Eugenia's cow was a *moo*. However, day after day, encountering several different *moos* in the fields, village roads and in children's books, he developed a generic understanding of the concept *moo*: every time he would see a cow, he would point to it with his finger and try to imitate the sound.

Semantic memory is deduced from experience by noting the

common features of many different experiences. It does not develop all at once but requires repetition. As a rule, we say that children have acquired a semantic memory for the concepts of *cow*, *house* and *car*, if they no longer remember the circumstances in which they learned about cows, houses and cars. Because semantic memory is of enormous importance in everyday life, many models have been proposed to describe its organization. Some of them are multi-purpose models attempting to explain a wide range of cognitive abilities (such as language use, decision-making and reasoning), whereas others deal only with semantic memory. Here I shall limit myself by briefly describing two main types of semantic memory models: feature comparison models and network models.

In feature comparison models of semantic memory, a particular concept is represented in memory as combination of semantic features and attributes. One of the most popular feature comparison models, proposed by the psychologist Edward Smith of Stanford University, divides features into two sets: *defining* features and *characteristic* features.[19] So a concept such as 'bird' would have the following subset of features: wings, feathers, beak, song, flight, food for foxes, and so on. Of those, 'wings' is a defining feature because all birds have wings. But 'song', while being a characteristic feature of birds, is not a defining feature because some birds have it, others don't. Similarly, egg-laying may be a characteristic feature of all birds, but it is not a defining feature because it also applies to reptiles, insects and fishes.

According to the model, people compare the attributes of an item with those stored in long-term memory for a concept. Recall is quicker when there is either low or high correspondence of features than when there is a moderate overlap between the item and the concept stored in long-term memory. You are more likely to answer 'yes' without giving a second thought to the question, 'Is a robin a bird?' than to the question, 'Is a penguin a bird?' That is because a penguin, one of the prettiest creatures in the world, does not have many of the characteristic features of birds: it does not fly, nor can it sing, and, fortunately, it is not on a fox's menu. In such case recall will be postponed until you check some of the defining features (wings, feathers). However, the problem with the model is that not all concepts have precisely defining features (for example, a bed or a table). Hence it cannot be applied to the broader issues of semantic processing.

In 1969, the computer scientist Ross Quillian and the psychologist Alan Collins proposed a network model of semantic memory (no idea in science is ever entirely new; this model can find precursors in the writings of Aristotle).[20] The nice thing about their model is that it is mentally *economical*. Let me explain this. The model assumes that information is stored in a hierarchically arranged network of interrelated concepts. Each concept is stored as a node (by 'node', psychologists mean a neural network) and each node has a set of characteristic properties. These properties are stored at the highest level to which they generally apply. In other words, since all birds have wings, it is mentally more economical to attach this property to the general concept 'bird', than to attach it to every instance of a bird. Similarly, because all birds eat, 'eat' is attached to the highest concept: in this case, the concept 'animal'. Nonetheless, the fact that the model assumes that all links are equal in strength, creates problems. If the link between, say, 'bird' and 'robin' in the model is equivalent to a link between 'bird' and 'penguin', why do we take longer to decide that a penguin is a bird than that a robin is a bird?

Puzzled by this sort of problem, Alan Collins and the psychologist Elizabeth Loftus introduced a revised version of the model.[21] They abandoned a strict hierarchical association of semantic concepts and proposed the existence of different kinds of links between concepts. Most notably, they suggested that each concept is associated with brain activity that is spread from one concept to the next until the two concepts are linked. In its simplest form the spreading activation model assumes that because 'cat' and 'mouse' are associated, presenting one concept (cat) will lead to excitation flowing to the other (mouse), which in turn will lead to its quicker identification. The problem, however, is that all these theories neglect the crucial link between the concepts and the world outside the semantic network. The environment in which we live has a vital effect on the way in which we remember. Whether powerful or flexible, these models may not really portray how we actually act in the real world.

What Colour is a Mouse?

The dissociation of episodic and semantic memory systems is dramatically illustrated by studies of amnesic patients. Remembering the colour of a mouse, a cherry or an eggplant requires the operation of a different brain network from that used to remember one's honeymoon or summer holidays. Recognizing a briefcase seems to depend on different neural machinery from that used in recognizing a daffodil. Each of these kinds of information depends on the integrity of specific brain structures and underlying neural function. Let me begin with the case of L.P., an intelligent forty-four-year-old secretary, described by the Italian neurologists Emilio De Renzi, Mario Liotti and Paolo Nichelli in 1987.[22] This patient developed brain damage following infection of the brain by a strain of herpes virus, a dangerous virus that is the main cause of encephalitis in Western societies. The damage was primarily confined to the front portion of the temporal lobe, which is positioned just over the ears, and is essential for semantic memory (Figure 3). The patient's semantic memory deficit was devastating. She no longer remembered the meanings of common words, she lost virtually all her memories of historical events and famous people, geographical knowledge and knowledge of social customs, and most of her knowledge of the attributes of animate and inanimate objects, their smells, colours and textures. She could not identify the colour of a mouse, or where to look for soap. Remarkably, however, she did have vivid and accurate recollections of her engagement and honeymoon, her father's death, her children's births, and many other incidents from her past. She was a woman with a personal history but no general knowledge of the world. Similarly, elderly patients with a memory disorder called *semantic dementia* show severe deficits in semantic knowledge of words, concepts and objects. They may not identify a picture of a deer, but they have no problem in remembering where they spent a recent holiday. This evidence indicates that even if most semantic memories disappear, episodic memories can remain well preserved.

Some particularly intriguing cases provide important clues as to how our general knowledge of the world is organized in the brain. In 1984 the British neuropsychologists Elizabeth Warrington and Tim Shallice reported the cases of four encephalitic patients who had also become victims of a herpes virus.[23] The virus left all four patients with semantic memory problems. Although all the patients had great difficulty recognizing living things, they easily identified most inanimate objects. One of the patients, known by the initials J.B.R., could describe manufactured objects such as a briefcase – 'small case used by students to carry papers'. But he had difficulty with animate objects – a daffodil was a 'plant', and an ostrich was 'unusual'. So semantic memory may indeed be hierarchically organized, as Collins and Quillian proposed. When the system is damaged, the ability to access the lower and more detailed nodes of the semantic memory is grossly reduced, but the subject still appears to be able to move up to higher-level concepts. Memories of flowers might be gone, but memories of plants remain.

Golf with Frederick

While some amnesic patients do not remember the colour of a mouse but recollect their summer holidays, others have perfect memories of golf jargon but do not recall any specific trips to the golf course.

Frederick, a passionate golf-player in his mid-fifties, was accepted at the unit for memory disorders at the University of Toronto in 1981. He was studied by Daniel L. Schacter, at that time a predoctoral psychologist, and now a professor at Harvard. Schacter immediately noticed that there was something dreadfully wrong with Frederick's memory. Frederick did not remember how he had made his way to the clinic for testing or what he had done the day before. He had stopped working, and led a quiet life with no plans for the future and nothing to look forward to.[24]

Frederick's memory problems were not caused by encephalitis or a motorcycle accident. He had a devastating memory illness – Alzheimer's disease. In the advanced stages of Alzheimer's disease virtually all cognitive systems are disrupted. But when the disease is in its earlier stages, as it was in Frederick's case, it is possible to detect selective impairments of some cognitive processes against a background of otherwise normal cognition. Sometimes, only one or a very few systems are affected over many years.

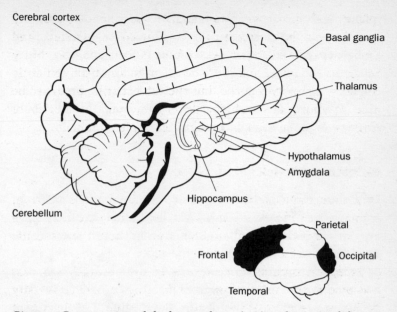

Figure 3 Cross-section of the human brain (top), and its main lobes (bottom)

'Why not study memory systems and play golf at the same time?' thought Schacter. After all, Frederick seemed to provide the perfect opportunity. Equipped with a tape recorder, the young psychologist therefore invited Frederick to a game. The fairways and greens became a natural laboratory. Every time Frederick used some golf jargon, Schacter recorded what it was and whether it was adequately and appropriately used. To Schacter's best estimation, Frederick's golf vocabulary was excellent – words such as *birdie*, *dog-leg*, *wedge* and *finesse shot* were used by the patient as meaningfully as any other golfer would use them. Frederick's access to his memory of the procedural and strategic aspects of game was perfect too. He would use a coin to mark the location of a ball (a standard procedure among golfers) and he would select the proper clubs. However, after each round, when the partners had drinks in the clubhouse, Frederick was unable to recollect a single episode from the entire round. Not surprisingly, when Schacter invited him to play again a week later, Frederick commented that he was a 'bit nervous, because he had not been playing golf for several months.' Frederick's episodic memory evaporated like camphor!

Memories of *How*, *That* and *Others*

Even though the evidence suggests that semantic and episodic memories can be dissociated, the border between these two memory systems seems rather fragile. Both involve the knowledge of facts, whether semantic or episodic; both can be brought to mind; and both can be declared. So semantic and episodic memories found their shelter under the title *declarative* memory, thanks to the Californian scientists Neal J. Cohen and Larry R. Squire.[25] According to Squire, declarative memory is what is usually meant when we say 'memory' in ordinary language. The term *explicit* memory, suggested by Schacter, has a similar meaning.

What does it do? Here is a simple 'on-line' example. When you read this book, your declarative memory system supports your ability to understand it, to recall the book or at least some of its content, figures, phrases or references. You might remember where and when you bought the book, or that you were reading the book in a plane while travelling from London to New York. Finally, your declarative memory supports the flexible use and manipulation of the information stored about the book in your long-term memory. It will help you to compare it with other books written on memory, to give plausible or critical accounts of it, or even to use it to pick up some citations and references.

All of our memories of knowing facts and events are supported by a declarative memory system. We know that Moscow is the capital of Russia, and Gorbachev is the man who initiated *perestroika*; we may remember that NATO began an air strike against Yugoslavia on 21 March 1999; we know that Hitler was a monster, and so was Stalin; we know that Leonardo da Vinci was a genius, and so was Mozart; we remember that we had a blue-and-red bicycle when we were seven, and so did the boy next door.

However, we also remember *how* to ride a bicycle, *how* to swim and *how* to play golf (assuming we have ever learned all these). All these memories of *how* are within the scope of *procedural* memory system. Procedural memories benefit from repetitions and, with extensive practice of behavioural routines and habits, can be run on autopilot. We know from experience that once we have mastered the art of swimming, bicycling, skiing or skating, we no longer need much conscious thought. The term 'procedural memory' was originally used to contrast with 'declarative memory' (both terms were borrowed from the field of artificial intelligence). However, it soon became clear that certain memories that are not declarative are not well accommodated by the term 'procedural' either. Scientists have been intrigued to discover that much of what we retrieve from memory may be hidden from our conscious awareness. The central question is therefore: are we always aware that we are remembering?

Whether or not we show retention of memory depends more on the type of testing technique used than on the type of knowledge being processed. While one technique detects no evidence of memory, another one, of more sophisticated design, will testify to its existence. As Steven Rose says, 'Memory is often not so much lost as hard to find.'

In the late 1960s, beginning with the seminal work of the

British psychologists Elizabeth Warrington and Lawrence Weiskrantz, several articles about amnesic patients have reported some intriguing and puzzling findings.[26] The researchers designed a procedure in which amnesic patients and normal volunteers studied some common words, such as *hotel*, *absence*, *juice* or *telephone*. Some of these words were then mixed with new words and shown again later. Amnesic patients had great difficulty recognizing which words they had seen before on the list and which they had not. You probably wonder what is intriguing or puzzling about this. It was already known from previous reports that amnesic patients had problems remembering words from a recently presented study list. The surprise came, however, after Warrington and Weiskrantz made a small but ingenious modification in their testing technique. They now presented the first three letters of a word, such as 'abs—' or 'tel—', and asked subjects to supply the absent letters. Impressively, amnesic patients could play the game almost as well as people with normal memory. But something else was interesting about the patients' performance: they had no idea that they were recalling words from the previously seen list. They were remembering some aspects of a recent experience, even though they had no awareness of it. This was memory without remembering. This kind of learning is called *priming*.[27] What seems to be happening during priming is that the patient's behaviour alters as a result of recent experience and this altered behaviour outlasts the patient's memory of the experience itself.

Although research into priming exploded relatively recently, early examples of retention without awareness in amnesic patients can be found in the writings of the British physician Robert Dunn in 1845, and in those of the French philosopher Henry Bergson and the French physician Edouard

Claparede in 1911.[28] Claparede described the case of a forty-seven-year-old woman suffering from Korsakoff's syndrome, a brain disease caused by severe alcoholism that leaves its victims with even blanker memory records than Frederick's or L.P.'s. As an experiment, Claparede shook his patient's hand and at the same time jabbed it with a pin hidden between his fingers. A few minutes later the patient no longer remembered the event – or even the doctor. However, when Claparede reintroduced himself and reached out for her hand, she pulled it back. When he asked her for a reason, she replied, 'Does not one have the right to withdraw one's hand?' But when he pressed her further, she said, 'Is there perhaps a pin hidden in your hand?' And she added, 'That was an idea that went through my mind.' Claparede's patient showed no conscious memory of the pinprick episode, and yet she acted as though she had stored some knowledge of this episode.

Such separation between two kinds of knowledge represents a particularly extreme case of a relatively normal phenomenon of memory. We retain knowledge that we have acquired on a particular occasion long after we have forgotten the episode itself. We experience priming in everyday life. A good idea pops up in our mind, unattached to any context or experience; we do not remember reading about it anywhere or discussing it with a colleague or a friend; and we assume that we have come up with it just now, only later to realize that it was derived from specific experience. Priming may occur under hypnosis, and sometimes even under anaesthesia. The cases of unintentional plagiarism (also called cryptomnesia) in music, art and literature, not to say science, may also result from priming. Writers have long tried to explain this peculiar tendency. It is best described in Mark Twain's own words in *Innocent Plagiarism*:

I had really stolen that dedication almost word for word. I could not imagine how this curious thing had happened... However, I thought the thing out and solved the mystery. Two years before, I had been laid up a couple of weeks in the Sandwich Islands and had read and re-read Doctor Holmes's poems till my mental reservoir was filled up with them to the brim. The dedication lay on the top, and handy, so by and by I unconsciously stole it. Perhaps I unconsciously stole the rest of the volume too, for many people have told me that my book was pretty poetical in one way or another.

Psychologists have now invented a variety of games to test priming in people. For instance, if a word is flashed in front of you for about five-hundredths of a second, it will be difficult to name the word, because the exposure time is so short. But if you had seen the word a day or two before, you would have more chance of naming it correctly. Your ability to say the right word indicates that a prior episode can influence future behaviour even though you do not recollect the episode. It seems that memory, and conscious awareness of it, can readily be separated. Several researchers have claimed that these findings provide excellent evidence for distinct memory systems in the brain.

The question now arose as to how to categorize this hidden world of memories. Most of them are not procedural, nor do they require awareness for recollection – so they are not declarative either. What more evidence does one need to invent new terminology? Consequently, all the memories that reveal themselves in the absence of awareness have been named by Peter Graf and Daniel Schacter as 'implicit memories'.[29] But clearly the collection of all our memories cannot be simply subserved by a single brain structure. What, then, are these brain structures that subserve the hidden world of our memories? And what are those that allow us to declare, 'I want to thank my brain for remembering me?'[30]

The Early Search for the Engram

Memories are not shackles, Franklin, they are garlands. *Alan Bennett*

Is memory actually stored somewhere in our brain, and, if so, where? The hunt for the location of memory has often been referred to as the 'search for the engram'. An engram is the term used to describe the memory trace that is presumably present in the brain after something has been learned. No one has ever seen it, but many believe it exists. Historically, there has been considerable debate about whether specific engrams are located in specific areas of the brain or distributed throughout the entire brain.

The modern era of the localization of different regions of the cerebral cortex (a folded layer of grey matter that contains about seventy per cent of our brain cells and covers the two cerebral hemispheres; *see* Figure 3) dates back to the late eighteenth century and begins with a Viennese psychologist, Franz Joseph Gall, the founder of phrenology – the doctrine of the correlation of the size and shape of skull bumps with personality.[31] Gall had a successful reputation in Germany, England and the United States, and his ideas were fashionable among many distinguished intellectuals, including Honoré de Balzac, George Eliot and A. R. Wallace. But he was ridiculed by the leading French physiologist of the day, Pierre Flourens, later professor of natural history at the Sorbonne. A technically superb experimenter, Flourens attempted to disprove Gall's ideas by an experiment in which he removed portions of the brains of live pigeons to see what happened to their behaviour. After two decades of painstaking research he reported that although lesions of the cerebral hemispheres had devastating effects on remembering and perceiving, the site of damage was irrelevant – all regions of the hemisphere contributed to these functions. His conclusion – that the brain operated as a single unit – was an over-simplification, but it helped to refute Gall's theory of phrenology.

Although phrenology had nothing to say about single versus multiple memory systems, Gall's ideas stimulated the search for correlations between the site of brain injury and specific psychological defects in humans as well as experimental animals. The debate about localization reached a peak in 1861 at the April meeting of the Paris Société d'Anthropologie when Paul Broca, a professor of pathology at the Sorbonne and founder of the society, announced that he had critical findings on this issue. Broca reported the autopsy results of a patient who had long-standing language problems. The patient was nicknamed by his fellow patients 'Tan' because 'tan' was the only word he could say. Tan's incapacity to speak, Broca argued, was the consequence of a specific, distinct lesion, about the size of an egg, in the left frontal lobe of his brain. The frontal lobes, rising just behind the forehead, are the biggest and evolutionarily the newest of our four cerebral lobes – the occipital, frontal, temporal and parietal lobes. Although Tan's linguistic abilities appeared to be grossly impaired, his loss was limited, Broca claimed, to memory of the procedures required for articulating words. This epochal discovery identified a particular area of the brain, now known as Broca's area, with the distinctive function of verbal expression.[32]

The doctrine of localization of function was further shaped in 1874, when the German neurologist Carl Wernicke found another region on the left side of the cerebral hemisphere, known today as Wernicke's area, that controlled the recognition of different aspects of language. Broca's area, as

Wernicke explained, regulates coordinated movements of speech, while Wernicke's area embodies the auditory records of individual words. In general, Wernicke believed that there was plenty of space in the cerebral cortex to accommodate different memories:

> The cerebral cortex with its 600 millions of cells...offers a sufficiently great number of storage places in which the innumerable sensory impressions provided by the outer world can be stored one by one without interference. The cerebral cortex is populated with such residues of past stimuli, which we propose to call memory.[33]

The technique of removing parts of the brains of live animals, used by Flourens, was a successful one and was adopted by many investigators in the hope of finding a memory trace. One such investigator was Karl Lashley, the distinguished physiological psychologist, the 'godfather' of the engram hunters, who in 1946 summed up the results of his thirty-three-year odyssey to find the memory trace:

> It is not possible to demonstrate the isolated localization of a memory trace anywhere within the nervous system. Limited regions may be essential for learning or retention of a particular activity, but within such regions the parts are functionally equivalent. The engram is represented throughout the region...I sometimes feel, in reviewing the evidence on the localization of the mory trace, that the necessary conclusion is that learning just is not possible.[34]

Why and how did he come to such a conclusion?

Lashley trained rats to run different mazes. Before or after training, he gradually removed portions of cortex, and tested

the effects of these ablations on initial learning or postopera-
tive memory. Sooner or later, he hoped, his scalpel would cut
the magic piece of tissue that stores memory, and then his
animals would suddenly have no maze-running knowledge.
Instead, to his surprise and disappointment, he found that
rats with massive holes in their cortex were stumbling and
hobbling, but nevertheless performing well on the maze
tasks. Although the operations interfered with their performance, no part of the cortex seemed to matter more than any
other. The impairments were more or less proportional to the
amounts of tissue removed: if a small piece of cortex was
destroyed, the loss was scarcely detectable; if large parts were
removed, the memory of the task was lost.

Lashley's results suggested that the amount of cortical
tissue destroyed was far more important than the location of
the damage. On the basis of these and similar experiments
performed on monkeys, Lashley was forced to conclude that
the engram did not reside in any place in particular. Re-
luctantly, he rejected his original idea that specific memories
are stored in specific regions of the brain, and instead he
formulated a concept of *equipotentiality*. Equipotentiality,
according to Lashley, is the ability of any intact part of a functional region to carry out functions lost by the destruction of
other parts. There are no special places in the brain reserved
for specific memories: memories are diffusely distributed
throughout the brain. In other words, they are simultaneously
everywhere and nowhere. But as Lashley was reaching his
bitter conclusion, one of the great breakthroughs in memory
science, which eventually dismissed this view, was being
made by Canadian neurologists.

Chapter 3

The Wiring of a Sea Horse: What is the Hippocampus For?

Who is it that can tell me who I am? William Shakespeare

Dr William Scoville was not searching for the memory trace when he performed his historic operation at the Hartford Hospital, Connecticut, on a summer morning in 1953. The neurosurgeon hoped that the brain areas he removed from a twenty-seven-year-old patient would help to ease the patient's severe and recurrent epileptic seizures. Sadly, this clinical experiment did not cure the epilepsy (although it did reduce the severity of the seizures). Instead, it created a man with devastating memory problems, the patient ever since known as H.M., who has arguably become the single most studied and quoted patient in the history of medical literature. His peculiar memory deficit stimulated much modern research on conscious and unconscious memories, and triggered a renaissance in memory science. What had happened to H.M. that made him so tragically special?

Scoville removed from H.M. a complex of brain structures packed deep within the inner surface of the temporal lobes on both sides of the brain, just over the ears. The package of structures included most of the hippocampus (the Greek word for 'sea horse'), the amygdala (Greek for 'almond'), and some neighbouring areas of temporal cortex. It was immediately clear following the surgery that there was something wrong, terribly wrong, with H.M.'s memory. Although he could speak, converse and read normally, he had no idea where he was, with whom he was speaking, or what he had read just a few minutes ago. He could not remember what he had had for breakfast or even whether he had recently eaten a meal; nor could he find his way to the bathroom, or recognize members of the hospital staff. It seemed as if his life after surgery was no longer contributing to his store of knowledge. It was as if he had lost an actual organ of memory.[1]

Nonetheless, H.M. was able to hold immediate impressions in his mind, just for a few seconds, or sometimes even for minutes. But as soon as his attention was distracted they were lost. What was interesting, however, was that old memory from his childhood was still intact. He remembered an old country house in South Coventry, with many rooms, and that his bedroom had a fireplace. He remembered taking swimming lessons in a public pool, playing cards for fun but not for money, and chasing squirrels with his father's gun behind the house in the woods. He recalled the trips in his teenage years to the lakes in New Hampshire and Canada, where he used to hunt and fish with his father. He remembered his girlfriend's name, Mildred, and even recalled, with a smile, how he dropped her for another, Beverly, just because she loved skating with him. So the surgical removal of H.M.'s inner structures of the temporal region had destroyed his memory of recent experiences while his general level of intelligence, immediate memory or very old memories were unharmed. Indeed, the crucial thing to realize here is that memory impairment in amnesic patients like H.M. is highly *selective*.

Flashbacks in the Temporal Lobe

In fact, H.M. was not the first patient to show this kind of selectivity in memory impairment. In the 1940s and 1950s, the Canadian neurosurgeon Wilder Penfield began to explore the brains of epileptic patients with thin-wired electrodes in order to pinpoint the regions responsible for seizures. Because this sort of manipulation is not painful, the patients could remain conscious during the entire procedure and guide the surgeon through the secret places of the brain. So, if Penfield probed a certain brain area and the patient heard voices, or instruments playing a melody, he knew that he was stimulating the auditory cortex. If, on the other hand, the patient's leg or hand jerked upward as a result of brain stimulation, he knew that he was touching a motor zone.

Penfield finally probed the temporal lobes. He knew from Hughlings Jackson's previous studies that epileptic discharges in the temporal lobes could induce some odd sensations – 'dreamy' states or the feelings of familiarity known as *déjà vu*. But what he found when he touched this brain region exceeded his expectations. The patients reported their *memories*. In Penfield's own words:

> They were electrical activations of the sequential record of consciousness, a record that had been laid down during the patient's earlier experience. The patient 're-lived' all that he had been aware of in that earlier period of time as in a moving picture 'flashback'.[2]

What does this mean? Could it be that memory is localized in the temporal lobes? Does this mean that Lashley's concept of diffuse distribution of memory throughout the brain was wrong?

The first answer came from Penfield's own work. He started to remove parts of the temporal or frontal lobe as a treatment for patients with localized injury-causing seizures. Parts were removed from one side of the brain and typically included the hippocampus, the amygdala and some portions of temporal cortex. Such operations, as Penfield and his colleague Brenda Milner found, caused only moderate memory impairments. However, Milner and Penfield soon encountered two patients with a severe and persistent deficit of recent memory, but no intellectual loss – just as in H.M.'s case – following removal of parts limited to the left temporal lobe. Why would the removal of only one side of the temporal lobe produce such a severe, generalized memory loss? Milner and Penfield believed that there must have been pre-existing damage in one (or more) of the crucial structures of the opposite brain side, so that when the surgeon cut one side of the temporal lobe, the other side could not take on the storage function. The hypothesis was right. Nine years later, when one of the patients (P.B.) died, autopsy findings revealed the existence of long-standing massive right hippocampal atrophy. Interestingly, the rest of the right temporal lobe, including the amygdala, showed no abnormality. The crucial structure must have been the hippocampus.

The Transitional Station

When Scoville heard about Milner's findings, he invited her to come to Connecticut to explore H.M.'s memory deficit. After all, H.M.'s memory problem seemed rather similar to that of Penfield's two patients, except that it was more severe. It is through Milner's extensive studies that H.M. became so well known. Here he is, as seen through the eyes of Milner and colleagues, fourteen years after the operation:

H.M.'s severe anterograde amnesia persists...He still fails to recognize people who are close neighbors or family friends but who got to know him only after the operation...Although he gives his date of birth unhesitatingly and accurately, he always underestimates his own age and can only make wild guesses as to the date...During three of the nights at the Clinical Research Center, the patient rang for the night nurse, asking, with many apologies, if she would tell him where he was and how he came to be there. He clearly realized that he was in a hospital but seemed unable to reconstruct any of the events of the previous day. On another occasion he remarked, 'Every day is alone in itself, whatever enjoyment I've had, and whatever sorrow I've had.' Our own impression is that many events fade for him long before the day is over. He often volunteers stereo-typed descriptions of his own state, by saying that it is 'like waking from a dream.' His experience seems to be that of a person who is just becoming aware of his surroundings without fully comprehending the situation, because he does not remember what went before.[3]

Importantly, H.M. also had some retrograde amnesia. In fact, when he was tested in the early 1980s, he did not recall any specific events from several years preceding his surgery, but he remembered many episodes that happened before his sixteenth birthday – the day he first developed severe seizures. This time window provided crucial early evidence for the consolidation hypothesis I introduced early in the book. It became clear that the medial temporal area is critical to memory only for a limited time. If so, and the medial temporal region is only a transitional station, where does memory transfer to? Because H.M. had no problem recalling his childhood and teenage experiences, it seems that these memories had passed through temporal lobe storage and become fixed somewhere else. Nobody can say for sure where exactly, but presumably these memories found their permanent store in the neighbouring cortical regions that survived the surgery.

The transitional role of the medial temporal region in memory was also illuminated by the fact that H.M., like other amnesic patients who have been carefully tested, had intact short-term memory capacity. Indeed, the selective memory deficit of these patients demonstrates a distinction between short-term and long-term memory similar to the one developed in experimental psychology. In one experiment, for example, five amnesic patients, including H.M., and twenty control subjects were presented with a sequence of five digits and asked to repeat it. If the subjects made an error, they were given the same string again until it was repeated correctly. If no error was made, one digit was added to the next sequence. Under these conditions, normal subjects could extend their span gradually up to twenty digits, mastering it in fewer than fifteen trials. The patient H.M. began with a normal digit span of six but was unable to extend it at all beyond this number even after extensive repetition. The same was true of the other patients. Clearly, the absence of the medial temporal region does not prevent the formation of short-term memory. Its absence becomes vital, however, when the task's demands exceed what can be held in short-term memory.

The intact capacity for short-term memory can also be demonstrated on tests with music. In the so-called 'seashore' tonal memory test a short melody of three to five notes is played twice in rapid succession and the subject's task is to guess which note is changed at the second playing (I believe that you need a good ear for music to detect this). Here again, H.M.'s performance was normal, and so was that of the amnesic patients P.B. and F.C., described by Penfield and Milner. Furthermore, H.M.'s failure to establish long-term memory traces did not seem absolute either. He seemed to learn something about the general arrangement of the rooms and furniture in his home. He also had islands of remembering, such as knowing that an astronaut is someone who 'travels in outer space', or that a 'public figure named Kennedy was assassinated' and that rock music is 'that new kind of music we have'.[3]

Learning Without Recollection

Can the same man know and also not know that which he knows? *Plato*

When amnesiacs such as H.M., Frederick and N.A. are tested in the laboratory rather than on their day-to-day experience, they show a cluster of similarly preserved capacities and skills. First, as we have already seen, very remote memory is spared, as is immediate memory. Invariably, it seems to be well documented that procedural memory does not suffer; the brain damage does not result in the loss of previously learned motor skills, nor does it prevent the acquisition of new motor skills. A second, striking and common feature is the discrepancy between the sparing of non-declarative memory and the loss of declarative memory. One example of this is a fascinating experiment with H.M. that required perceptual recognition skills.[4] The name of the test is the *Gollin incomplete pictures task*, first devised by Gollin for use with children, and later borrowed by Warrington and Weiskrantz. Instead of words, the test uses a series of incomplete drawings of objects and animals (for example an aeroplane or a butterfly; Figure 4). The whole test consists of twenty drawings, each presented in a series graded in difficulty from the sketchiest outline to the complete picture.

The game begins by presenting a subject with the most

difficult, fragmented figures. The subject is allowed to look at each drawing for a second and encouraged to guess what the sketchy figure might be. The procedure is continued through successive easier sets of drawings, until all pictures of a given series have been correctly identified. Milner and her team found that H.M. could play the game quite well, proving that his perceptual abilities, or priming, were within the normal range. He even showed some improvement on retest an hour later, although he had no idea of having taken the test before – a crystal-clear manifestation of learning without any conscious recollection.

Further studies established that the domain of preserved learning in amnesia extends beyond perceptual and motor skills to cognitive skills as well. Like other amnesiacs, H.M. could demonstrate a steady improvement in performance in a variety of fancifully named memory games – the Tower of Hanoi, the jigsaw puzzle, or the 'closure' task. Yet each time he was introduced to a given task he had no recollection of ever having seen or played it before. What non-declarative memory repeatedly testified, declarative memory continued to deny.

Nowadays this does not seem a surprise: those who work with memory are well aware that such dissociation is possible following a discrete brain lesion. But for scientists, looking at this finding for the first time, it was quite extraordinary. Is it possible that the person's memory is so destroyed that he can learn a skill without ever being aware of this? Is it possible that the person can rehearse a task from day to day, indeed master it, without any idea that this is in fact what is happening? What is the explanation? Is it possible that the person has two different minds, one of them remembering what the other has forgotten? It sounds strange, and yet this is a typical feature of the type of memory loss that occurs with such brain damage. The inevitable conclusion is that non-

Figure 4 Incomplete pictures task

declarative and declarative memory are stored in different areas of the brain, so that declarative memory can be destroyed while non-declarative memory is unimpaired. The long-standing philosophical question raised by Plato – 'Can the same man know and also not know that which he knows?' – seems to have found a scientific answer.

Things are far more complicated, however. Non-declarative memory appears to play its own tricks. Nelson Butters and his colleagues at the University of California School of Medicine at San Diego, California, found that learning motor skills (for example, making drawings or exercises) recruits a rather different memory system than does priming. Butters' team studied patients with Huntington's disease – the genetically transmitted disorder that destroys the brain's motor system – and compared them with patients with Alzheimer's disease. In Huntington's disease, damage is largely restricted to a set of deeply located brain structures known as the basal ganglia, which are critical in the learning of sequential body movements. In Alzheimer's disease, however, it is the medial temporal lobes and other cortical areas that become gradually ruined. Consequently, as we have already seen in the case of

Schacter's golfing partner Frederick, patients show a profound deficit in declarative memory. Researchers found that whilst patients with Huntington's disease show good priming on a word-completion test but have difficulty in acquiring new motor skills, Alzheimer's patients have no difficulty acquiring motor skills but show a severe loss of priming. These findings demonstrated convincingly that priming and skill learning depend on separate brain structures.

In the years following Scoville's and Milner's pioneering work, H.M.'s case was often cited to support the idea that recent declarative memory depends on the hippocampus. But because the hippocampus was only one of several structures removed from H.M.'s medial temporal lobe, his case could not shed light on whether hippocampal damage alone was responsible for severe memory loss. Clearly, if the role of the various structures of the temporal lobe were to be understood, an animal model was needed.

Monkeys With Most Toys

Memory-less animals do not appear in clinics after motor-cycle accidents or aircraft crashes, nor do they become the victims of their room-mate's foolish fencing-foil games, like the human amnesiacs described above. Scientists in the laboratories produce animal models of human amnesia. Such experimental work can combine anatomical, physiological, biochemical and behavioural studies. Colourful chemicals that flow along axons, the slender 'wires' through which neural cells (neurons) send signals, have revealed the neural circuitry that might enable specific structures to play a role in memory. Recordings of the electrical activity of individual cells in the brains of awake animals have distinguished parts of the brain that are active during mental exercises.

Measurements of the sugar consumption by neural cells as animals memorize mazes have highlighted regions of the brain that are busy during learning. Another popular experimental approach has combined surgical removal of specific brain structures with psychological testing. The neural structures of experimental animals are destroyed and animals are then studied to solve tasks that allow scientists to tease apart the various components of memory and establish which one of them is impaired.

In 1978, the neuroscientist Mortimer Mishkin of the National Institute of Mental Health in Bethesda, reported a model of human amnesia in monkeys.[6] Mishkin and his colleagues aimed to identify the structures and pathways in the brain that underlay a monkey's ability to recognize objects. In Mishkin's test, called 'non-matching to sample', the monkey is shown a small toy for a few seconds, and shortly after is shown the same toy, plus a new one. To obtain a peanut or a banana pellet as a reward, the monkey has to keep in mind a simple puzzle – to recognize an old toy but to choose a new one. In a more sophisticated version of the test, developed by David Gaffan of the University of Oxford, a monkey's memory can be taxed by introducing a delay between the initial display and the choice. The power of this test is that researchers can manipulate the delays to tease apart memory components; if the delay between the first toy and the choice is very short and animals can do the task well, then one can say with confidence that the monkeys suffered no defect in visual perception or immediate memory. If, however, a researcher increases the delay up to a few minutes and the monkeys fail to perform the task, then this would be a good indication of true loss of long-term memory. Mishkin and his co-workers found that the removal of either the hippocampus or the adjacent amygdala had a very small effect on a monkey's ability to recognize which toy had been presented earlier, presumably because each brain structure can substitute for the other. But by damaging *both* structures together, the researchers created an animal model of global amnesia: the monkeys were as forgetful as the patient H.M., even though they could pick up the rules of the task and had no defect in visual perception.

The original work by Mishkin did not settle matters all at once. The question of precisely which structures within the medial temporal lobe were important for memory was still open. The brain structures described so far were revealed by their contribution to one kind of memory – recognition memory, in which a monkey, having seen a distinctive object only once, can recognize it many minutes later. In perceiving an object, however, one learns not only its distinguishing features, such as colour, size, shape or texture, but also its location with respect to other objects or landmarks. Remembering your car seems intuitively different from remembering where you parked it.

Could it be that neuroanatomically the task is different as well? Could it be that different neural pathways are specialized for different attributes of memory, say for remembering size, shape or spatial location? Indeed, further exploration has revealed interesting specialization in the two memory structures: although the hippocampus and the amygdala can substitute for each other in learning to recognize an object *per se*, the hippocampus seems to be crucially important for learning spatial relationships. This did not come as much of a surprise: 'monkey researchers' had already had some hints from 'rodent investigators' that suggested that the hippocampus is important for spatial learning. With this in mind, John K. Parkinson, working in Mishkin's laboratory, challenged normal monkeys to a spatial memory game.[7] In each round of the game the animals were shown two new objects in specific locations; shortly after, the monkeys were shown one of the original objects in its original location and an exact duplicate, either where the second object had been or in a new position. The monkeys were rewarded for choosing the original object in its original position. Once they mastered the task, they were transported to an operating room, where some of them were destined to lose forever their amygdala, and others their hippocampus.

Monkeys with no amygdala quickly relearned the task and did it accurately. It is now known that the damage to the amygdala alone does not seriously affect declarative memory (although it does play a key part in emotional memory). A lesion restricted to the hippocampus, however, left monkeys unable to perform the spatial memory task. At that time, a number of neuropsychologists argued that the hippocampus was a crucial structure underlying the declarative memory for recent experiences in humans, monkeys and other animals, and Parkinson's findings on spatial memory seemed to fit well into this concept. And yet, there have been extensive and often animated disputes about whether damage to the hippocampus alone is responsible for significant impairments in memory.

Soon two more amnesic patients were described, R.B. and G.D., who following temporary loss of blood-oxygen flow to the brain, had damage restricted to the particular region in the hippocampus known as the CA1 field.[8] Their memory impairments were similar in trend to H.M.'s memory loss, although milder. Much to the satisfaction of the 'hippocampus campus', these observations left no doubt that even partial destruction of the structure can cause notable memory loss.

But if damage to the hippocampus alone produces only

mild memory loss and damage to the amygdala alone has no effects on memory at all, why would combined damage to these two structures cause global amnesia? The first clue came from experiments in which researchers used more elegant and precise lesion techniques than those used previously.[9] Apparently, to produce global amnesia, one has to damage not only the hippocampus, but also the adjacent, anatomically related cortex (the entorhinal, perirhinal and parahippocampal cortices), a main source of input for the hippocampus and the amygdala.

The second clue came from a recent magnetic resonance imaging (MRI) study of H.M. This imaging method exploits the fact that atoms of individual molecules of the brain (as well as other organs or tissues) start to behave like little bar magnets or compass needles when subjected to a magnetic field. By skilfully manipulating them in a magnetic field, it is possible to line the atoms up, just as the needle of a compass lines up in the earth's magnetic field. When radio-wave pulses are applied to a brain whose atoms have been so aligned, the brain will emit detectable radio signals that are characteristic of the number of particular atoms present and their chemical environment. Brain images can be reconstructed by using the emission of radio signals from protons – particles that are abundant in the human body and have good magnetic properties. The resulting images of the brain are astonishingly beautiful and surpass in detail those produced by regular X-rays. The images obtained from H.M. indicated clearly that the severity of his memory deficit depended not only on his hippocampal damage but also on the fact that the surgical damage included the hippocampal region together with the neighbouring cortical areas. These cortical areas were intact in cases of moderate amnesia as seen in R.B. and G.D.[10]

Do I Know You?

I never forget a face, but in your case I'll make an exception.
Groucho Marx

What seems to be a modest memory deficit to a neuropsychologist's eye may be a frustrating experience for the patient. By 'modest', the neuropsychologist really means that the brain damage does not result in an across-the-board reduction of memory abilities. For example, it is possible that one can see and read perfectly well, but can no longer recognize objects and people. Or a person might recognize people and objects, but lose the ability to read or speak. Memory failures might reach such an extreme that one might even mistake the doctor for a dog, the maid for a table, or even one's wife's head for a hat.[11] Similar cases, brilliantly described in the writings of the neurologist Oliver Sacks, suggest that the competences of reading, seeing or recognizing objects and people are carried out by different structures in the brain. This, however, does not imply that these abilities are separate from beginning to end.

To explain such memory failures, many neuropsychologists adopted an 'information processing' approach. According to this view the information flows through a set of a distinct but interconnected neural networks (modules), each of which performs a particular job. These interconnected networks allow information to be processed in a parallel fashion so that damage to one part of the network does not necessarily affect the function of the rest of the system. It is like a fancy telephone system consisting of a number of interconnected components: a speaker, an answering machine, a voice scrambler and so on. For example, the speaker on my telephone has recently broken, but I can still make calls and receive recorded messages.

Independent defects in processing different aspects of visual information may result in highly selective impairments. Some people have difficulty in perceiving different tones of red, others movement or arrangement of objects in three-dimensional space. In some cases, brain damage can leave a person unable to recognize a human face while other visual skills remain intact. Somehow, the mechanisms in the brain for recognizing faces become cut off from conscious awareness.[12] This condition is known as prosopagnosia, from the Greek *prosopon* (face) and *agnosis* (without knowledge). Prosopagnosic people can tell that they are looking at a face, and they can recognize and describe separate features, such as the eyes, nose and mouth; some of them can even determine the age, sex and expression of the face. But to identify *whose* face they are looking at, or whether they have seen it before, is another matter. They cannot recognize the countenances of much-publicized rich and famous people, or photographs of 'wanted' criminals. In extreme cases, individuals will fail to recognize family members and close friends, or even their own face reflected in a mirror. Deprived of such capacities, they might recognize acquaintances by supplementary hints: context, body build or tone of voice.

Here is a less dramatic example from my own experience. Just yesterday, when I was in an elevator on my way home from the laboratory, a woman, perhaps a colleague, stepped into it on the fourth floor. She looked at me and asked, 'How are you?' 'I'm OK,' I answered, a bit confused and surprised because she clearly was not giving me just the trivial 'How ya doing?' but mistaking me for somebody else. I then paused, and asked, 'Do I know you?' Now she was the one who was confused, saying slightly embarrassedly, 'I thought you were Dr Laura from the eighth floor, but now when I hear your voice I realize that I was wrong.' I wonder if she had not heard my voice, would she continue to think she had seen Dr Laura?

Such experiences are common. We see a person on the street, but cannot 'place' him or her. We try desperately to decide whether we should approach the person and say hello. Are we acquainted personally, is the person a colleague, or someone we have seen last night on the television news? Perhaps later we realize that it was a cashier from a supermarket where we frequently shop. It seems that in such cases of 'mild prosopagnosia' there is a transient blockage in the brain's mechanism responsible for recognizing faces. This sort of incomplete functioning is intriguing, because our memory for faces is normally highly accurate: we have little difficulty identifying tens of thousands of people on sight.

But even for prosopagnosics, faces are forgotten but memories for faces are not totally lost. In 1984, Russell Bauer at the University of Florida described a man who was completely prosopagnosic. This patient could not place a correct name next to any photograph of a familiar face when he was given a choice of five alternative names. The truth, however, was found when Bauer recorded the electrical conductance of the patient's skin. This procedure – threateningly known as the lie detector test – is a sensitive measure of the amount of sweat produced by the skin in response to potentially upsetting questions. A sudden increase in skin conductivity indicates a nervous, emotional or guilty predisposition. Changes in skin responses were greater and more frequent when the patient chose the correct name rather than one of the four false names. Although Bauer's patient could not recognize familiar faces, he must have done so unconsciously at some level, given that his emotional response was different on seeing once-known faces. Recognition without awareness is called 'covert' recognition as opposed to 'overt' recognition, which refers to conscious recognition abilities.

Freda Newcombe and her co-workers at the neuropsychology unit of the Radcliffe Infirmary, Oxford, suggested that face recognition in the healthy brain is executed by a chain of subprocesses, some of which are not open to introspection. When this chain is broken, as happens with people after certain kinds of brain damage, some of these processes might continue to function normally, but the person is unaware of this because mechanisms later in the chain are damaged, disconnecting the intact processes from conscious awareness. To test this idea, Newcombe and Andrew Young of the department of psychology at the University of Durham designed an experiment, which involved familiar and unfamiliar faces but did not require overt identification of them. The first set of experiments was done with a patient called P.H., who lost his ability to recognize faces after suffering head injuries in a road accident.

As with any psychological experiment in humans or animals, a *control* experiment was first required. What if the patient had some vestigial awareness of familiar faces but lacked the confidence to acknowledge familiarity? To rule out this possibility the investigators presented P.H. with a large set of pairs of familiar and unfamiliar faces, such as Princess Diana and an unknown woman, Laurence Olivier and an ordinary man, and so on, and asked him to guess which one was a well-known face. The patient responded correctly on only fifty-one per cent of the trials – a clear indication of pure guessing, but nothing else. It seemed safe to say that he showed no sign of overt recognition.

After completing the control experiment, the real one began. The examiners aimed to detect covert face recognition and asked the patient to determine whether two photographs of faces presented together (e.g. Sylvester Stallone and Robert De Niro, and a pair of unknown faces) were of the same person or different people. And here is another example of the *control* experiment: when the researchers presented two pictures of the same person, they used photographs taken from different angles to avoid the possibility of the subject using pattern-matching rather than person-matching memory. The patient had no trouble sorting and matching familiar and unfamiliar faces as quickly as normal subjects, even though he could not identify any of the celebrities. Without going into a further description of this sophisticated experiment, it appeared that P.H.'s preserved abilities are similar to some aspects of recognition that operate automatically in normal people. Perhaps, suggests Newcombe, 'his covert face recognition stems from an intact face recognition system which has become disconnected from the processes that led to an awareness of recognition. Some of his face-recognition modules are preserved, but he has no conscious access to the outputs.'[13]

Good Guy, Bad Guy

Barring that natural expression of villainy which we all have, the man looked honest enough. *Mark Twain*

Antonio Damasio and colleagues at the University of Iowa also found a complete absence of overt learning, but signs of covert recognition, when their prosopagnosic patients were tested in the so-called 'good guy, bad guy' experiment.[14] One of the best-studied cases is that of the patient Boswell, a former newspaper advertising and printing salesperson, who has been observed in Damasio's laboratory since 1975. Boswell's disease was caused by a herpes virus, which severely damaged both temporal and frontal lobes. Not surprisingly, Boswell has a more profound memory deficit than the well-known H.M. The bigger holes in his brain seem to prohibit the retrieval of all episodic memories from any point of his life, regardless of how remote they were. His loss of memory for faces is painful: Boswell responded, 'That's my father,' to photographs of his father, a friend and himself. And yet, even against such complete absence of overt learning, he retained some sort of covert recognition. How was this discovered?

Damasio showed Boswell photographs of three different people, manipulating the emotional expression of each person. One person was designated as a 'good guy' and assumed a very positive, inviting posture, with a kind and smiling face; the second acted as a 'neutral guy', and the third played a 'bad guy': he had an angry face 'denying requests and favours'. A crucial factor in this experiment was the time Boswell was allowed to study the photographs: the 'good guy' picture was given minimal exposure time, while the 'neutral' and 'bad' guys could be observed and studied for as long as he liked. At no point after this experiment did Boswell admit that he had ever seen any of these faces before. When, however, he was presented with slides of these familiar faces together with unknown persons and asked to 'choose the person you like the best – who you would go to for rewards, treats and favours', Boswell demonstrated an intriguing recognition. In eighty-three per cent of cases he chose the familiar face of a 'good guy'. Clearly, Boswell did learn something about these individuals, although his learning was restricted to recognition of emotional expression and was not enough to permit face recognition. In Albert Camus's words, 'Charm is a way of getting the answer yes without having asked any clear question.' Such findings indicate that two different memory systems contribute to facial recognition: whilst the images of faces are stored in one part of the brain, the defining memories of each face might be stored in another. Perhaps, in times when we experience some momentary 'prosopagnosia', we have lost neither, but have difficulties in properly integrating the two.

However, the human brain seems to have some sort of temporal component for face recognition as well. In some instances, the access to memories of 'recent' faces might be blocked, while recognition of 'old' faces does not seem a troubling task at all.[15] In 1998, Larry Squire and his team compared amnesic patients with mild hippocampal lesions and patients with extensive temporal lobe damage on their ability to remember 'recent' and 'old' faces. They asked subjects to identify hundreds of photographs of famous people who came into the news in one of the decades from 1940 to 1995 (e.g. Elvis Presley for the 1960s, Ronald Reagan for the 1980s, Bill Clinton for the 1990s, and so on). Results of this study are astonishing. Whereas the patients with small hippocampal lesions (known to the scientific community as A.B. and L.J.) showed poor memory for the famous and rich people whose faces were currently on television screens and the front pages of newspapers, they remembered very well all the 'retro' celebrities. Meanwhile, for two other patients (known as E.P. and G.T.) with extensive brain damage, the faces of Clinton, Reagan or Presley were equally forgotten.

The implications of these extraordinary findings are considerable. They demonstrate that the hippocampus's role in holding memories of faces is time-limited: once the *faces* are transported into the surrounding structures of the brain and the surroundings are destroyed, memories are no longer accessible. Nonetheless, not accessible does not always mean not available. The distinction between availability and accessibility becomes more evident when healthy people are tested for their memory ability.

Recall versus Recognition

Somehow it seems common knowledge that our ability to *recognize* something is much better than our ability to *recall* the same thing. Take a minute and try to recall the names of the Corleone family from the film *The Godfather*. If you are like most people, you will have trouble recalling most of the names. If, on the other hand, you are presented with a list of a dozen names containing the names you failed to recall, you are likely to recognize them immediately. What is not *accessible* is, however, *available*.

Now suppose that you witness a crime. Perhaps it is a burglary, a shooting or a robbery. Regardless of the circumstances, you will form some memory trace of the lawbreaker that can have an important influence on the course of justice. Because you have seen the criminal, the police ask you to give the person's description. Although you have always thought of yourself as a good face-memorizer, you suddenly find yourself having difficulties in describing the criminal's face. A few days later you are called to the police station to identify the criminal. The police ask you to look at photo spreads or a line-up to indicate whether the person you saw on that fateful day is one of the people standing or pictured before you. 'It's him (or her)!' you exclaim. Thus, you are able to recognize the face that you failed to recall earlier, indicating that your memory became accessible. Of course, whether such eyewitness identification is accurate or not is another matter. It is now known that false identification occurs surprisingly frequently in staged-crime experiments. As Mark Twain noted, 'It is not so astonishing, the number of things that I can remember, as the number of things I can remember that are not so.'

Nonetheless, in less critical circumstances, our ability to register and recognize faces, names, objects or pictures is extremely good. Most of us, at one time or another, have experienced the irritated feeling that arises when we have been sweating at work all summer and a colleague who has just returned from a long holiday, tanned and relaxed, starts to show his holiday snaps. Despite the fact that we may only give these photos scant attention, we seem to remember them well. In one study, for example, healthy volunteers were shown 600 different coloured pictures. In a succeeding recognition test they were shown two pictures, one new and one seen earlier, and were asked to select the 'old' one – almost the opposite of the 'non-matching to sample' task that Mortimer Mishkin used when studying recognition abilities in monkeys. The subjects' recognition was phenomenal – they correctly picked out the 'old' pictures on ninety-seven per cent of trials.[16] Normally people can recall only about seventeen to twenty pictures. In a similar study, the Canadian psychologist Lionel Standing challenged the memory capacity of his volunteer subjects by presenting them with 2560 different slides, for a few seconds each, and testing later if they remembered them.[17] Again, subjects could accurately recognize almost all previously seen slides. It seems that nothing is forgotten, provided we know how to ask if it is remembered.

While psychological studies provide important evidence about the dissociation of recall and recognition, neuropsychological findings point to possible neural structures in the brain that might be responsible for these two distinct aspects of memory. As I mentioned above, people suffering from brain damage caused by an injury, tumour or stroke often lose certain brain functions without losing others. When Larry Squire and his co-workers were examining such patients on their ability to remember 'old' and 'recent' faces and events, they also noticed an interesting dissociation between recall and recognition. In their experimental design, the tests were administered first in a recall format. The subjects were asked, 'Who killed John Lennon?' and immediately afterwards they were given a recognition format test, consisting of four choices (e.g. John Hinkley, Sara Moore, David Roth, Mark Chapman). The patients with mild hippocampal damage performed poorly on recall tests (mainly recall of recent events). But they were almost as good as healthy subjects when they were checked on the recognition format test. Apparently, it is recall but not recognition that suffers when the key structure of the declarative memory system – the hippocampus – is destroyed. Yet even patients with extensive temporal lobe damage may sometimes show faint signs of recognition. But when their brains are taxed with demands that require recall rather than recognition, regardless of whether recall is of faces, facts or names, they have no clue.

The Tip-of-the-Tongue Experience

'Did somebody call me?' asked my son Irakli upon returning home.

Very confidently I began to report: 'Peter, Dan, Sara, and um…um…oh, it's on the tip of my tongue…um…It's K…um…'

'Ken?' he suggested, trying to help me.

'No, no,' I answered.

'Colin?'

'Yes, it's Colin, yes' – finally, with assistance, I managed to retrieve the name. Psychologists call these frustrating moments of name or word amnesia 'tip-of-the-tongue' phenomena. The correct answer seems just about to reach our conscious state but does not quite make it. Instead, recall is blocked, although partial information about the blocked name or word is often available. Such temporary loss in our ability to access information is an indication of retrieval failure, and is a good example of dissociation between the availability and the accessibility of memory.

The tip-of-the-tongue phenomenon is inherently interesting to most lay people and to memory researchers. Psychological questionnaire studies suggest that it is a nearly universal experience that occurs to everyone about once a week, and accelerates with age. The phenomenon often allows access to the target word's first letter and is frequently accompanied by words related to the target. For example, when we try to retrieve the word 'gooseberry', we often begin to helplessly mumble, 'blackberry, raspberry, strawberry...' Most of these annoying episodes are eventually successfully resolved, particularly if proper *retrieval cues* are supplied. Mentioning the correct response is a great retrieval cue because the person can recognize the correct answer (as happened to me with Colin's name). Similarly, if one has temporary evaporation of the word 'gooseberry', assistance with the category name 'berry' will be a good retrieval cue.

Speculations about the cause of the tip-of-the-tongue experience have centred on two mechanisms: *incomplete activation* and *blocking*. According to the incomplete activation viewpoint, the phenomenon is considered as a normal wordsearch process that has been drastically slowed because of insufficient target information. Deborah Burke and co-workers have argued that the retrieval problem occurs in the linkage between the phonological word systems and semantic word systems.[18] The meaning representation of a word usually allows direct and immediate access to its sound representation, thus enabling vocalization. But sometimes the phonological 'gate' is poorly activated, not allowing the linkage between the phonological word systems and semantic word systems to be established. As a result we feel confident that we know a word but we cannot retrieve it. So perhaps the increase in tip-of-the-tongue frequency in aged people results from the weakening of the semantic-phonological connection, which in turn reflects the reduction in subsidiary information about the target word (e.g. first letter, related words, category name) available to older people.

In contrast, the 'blocking' theory suggests that the tip-of-the-tongue experience represents a memory search that has become sidetracked to the wrong memory location. In the words of the psychologist Alan Brown, of the Southern Methodist University, Texas, 'tip-of-the-tongue experience reflects a memory search effort that took an inadvertent detour prior to the target and located an incorrect word.'[19] In these cases, the incorrect word diverts attention away from a word that we are trying to retrieve, and competes with it. As Freud speculated, when we are searching for a name, we often retrieve names that 'although immediately recognized as false, nevertheless obtrude themselves with great tenacity'. Some investigators label such words as *blockers*, whereas others have found more romantic names for them such as *interlopers*.

From a psycholinguistic perspective, it should not come as a surprise that we run into sporadic verbal gaps. According to Willem J. M. Levelt of the Max Planck Institute for Psycholinguistics in the Netherlands, turning the desired concepts into spoken words involves a complicated three-level process distributed throughout the memory stores.[20] Levelt calls the three levels the *lexical* network, the *lemma* network and the *lexeme* network. The lexical level handles thoughts and images. There we dip into our stored vocabulary – typically tens of thousands of words stored in vast interactive neuronal networks throughout the brain – activating all the information related to image (e.g. shape, size, colour, words related to image and so on). The activated concepts then pass to the next level, the lemma network, where the proper syntax is assigned to each concept. These are the rules of our language, including word order, gender if appropriate, case markings and other grammatical features. Finally, at the lexeme level, the mind has to match a chosen lexical concept to the proper combination of sounds that make up a language. This is where the process of generating concepts into speech can fail and a word will stick on the tip of the tongue.

However, failures may happen at any level. For example, one kind of speech error can occur in the transition of a thought between the lemma network and the lexeme network. Sometimes people – particularly children – exchange one word for another ('Fill up my tea with cup'), or mix up speech sounds ('bear' for 'hear'). Other types of errors might occur at lemma level when the various related concepts become engaged in a competition (e.g. gooseberry versus strawberry, blackberry, raspberry and so on). Eventually if we are not successful at finding the right word, we give up. Later, when we think again, the correct word often comes to mind. Waiting a few minutes gives the brain the time to 're-boot' its lexical concepts, speculates psychologist Gary Dell, so that the correct one can try again to win the competition.

The tip-of-the-tongue phenomenon has been extended to other senses as well. Sometimes, when people recall specific pictures, they might have a 'tip-of-the-eye' experience of a picture, in which their mental image is 'out of focus' and incapable of successfully retrieving a target image. Turning to a different sense, some people occasionally have a strong feeling that an odour is familiar, without being able to identify it. This is known as a 'tip-of-the-nose' experience. I am encountering it as I write this – there is a strong, familiar odour coming from my neighbour's kitchen, but I can't name it. Is it c..., um, c... – well, I won't worry too much; around sixty per cent of all 'tip-of' experiences are resolved within a minute of blocking.

It Will Rummage in Your Back Yard

I cannot tell what the dickens his name is. *William Shakespeare*

The brain seems to store information about names of people, objects, animals or places separately from all other information about them. For example, when I failed to retrieve Colin's name, I did, however, remember that he's a guy who studied with Irakli in Amherst, that they recently went together to Costa Rica, that he lives downtown and works in Wall Street. Similarly, we might forget for a while the name *gooseberry*, but we can say that what we want to name belongs to the category 'berry', that it can be green or red-brown in colour, that it's juicy and that it grows on bushes.

The idea of the existence of a 'separate store for names' draws support from psychological studies of reaction time.[21] In these experiments, people are presented with pictures and asked to make decisions about them as quickly as possible while researchers measure their reaction times. For instance, Andrew Young and his colleagues presented their subjects with a famous photograph (for example, a pop star or politician) and asked them either to name or to judge the person's profession. Naming took longer than judging the profession, even in the cases when the subjects had seen the pictures before. In similar experiments, Kathryn McWeeny and co-workers at the University of Lancaster obtained supporting evidence by using the same words sometimes as names and sometimes as occupational information. Apparently, it takes us longer to learn that a person's name is Mr Cook than to learn that a person is a cook.

To explain how brains might deal with names, the psychologists Mike Burton and Vicki Bruce at the University of Nottingham developed a computer model. The model consists of two clusters of units called 'person identity nodes' and 'semantic information units'. The idea is that there is one identity node for each person we know. When we see a person on the street, or recognize a person by hearing a voice, that person's unit becomes active, giving the first signals that 'the person is familiar'. But the activation is not sufficient to provide any further details. This happens at the second stage with the help of a second cluster of units, each of which contains some information about that person. So there will be units such as 'British', 'Russian', 'student', 'artist', 'singer' and so on. When any of these units reaches a certain level of activation, the appropriate information is retrieved.

The crucial part of the model is that each 'person' unit is connected to the information cluster. For example, the 'person' unit representing Paul McCartney is connected to units such as 'British', 'rock star', 'widower' and so on. But while certain details of personal information are common to many people, names are usually unique. This means that the units representing 'British' or 'rock star' are connected to many other people's units, whereas the unit identifying 'name is Paul McCartney' is linked to only one. So all information that is shared will become active more quickly than information that is unique. According to this scenario, what makes names relatively difficult to retrieve is not that they are stored separately from other information, but that they are generally unique.

While psychologists are concerned with *how* information is processed in the brain, neurologists are interested in *where* in the brain things happen. Recently, Antonio and Hanna Damasio came across two patients whose behaviour seemed to have some bearing on the issue of name retrieval.[22] The patients A.N. and L.R., who had sustained damage to the anterior and mid-temporal parts of the brain cortex, retained a normal ability to retrieve virtually all concepts. When shown pictures of human faces, body parts, animals, buildings, tools – to name just a few – both patients knew unequivocally what they were looking at. They could define an item's functions, value or history. But despite their indisputable knowledge, they could not retrieve the names of people or objects they knew very well. When the Damasios showed to A.N. a picture of Marilyn Monroe, he said, 'Don't know her name but I know who she is; I saw her movies; she had an affair with the President; she committed suicide; or maybe somebody killed her.' These patients did not suffer from prosopagnosia; they simply were unable to retrieve the name of the person they recognized. Similarly, when shown a picture of a racoon, they could recognize it without hesitation – 'It will come and rummage in your back yard and get into your garbage. The eyes and the rings in the tail give it away' – but they could not come up with the name. Other scientists have described patients with similar deficits. It seems that such patients experience a block between *retrieval of personal information* and *retrieval of names*. Curiously, nobody has observed a brain-damaged patient, or a healthy person, with the complementary deficit: good retrieval of names but blank memories for other personal details. The condition of losing the ability to name names is known as *anomic aphasia* (aphasia means partial or complete loss of ability to speak).

On the basis of extensive evidence from studies of people who had sustained brain damage, the Damasios proposed the hypothesis that our brain processes our thoughts into speech by means of three interacting sets of structures. First, a large collection of sensory and motor systems in both right and left hemispheres of the brain represents non-language interactions between the body and its environment: anything that we do, perceive, think or feel while acting in the world. Second, a few neural systems, generally located in the left cerebral hemisphere, represent words and sentences. A third set of structures, also located largely in the left hemisphere, mediates between the first two. Such triple structures, it seems to me, are places where Levelt's romantically named 'lemma–lexeme' processes may occur in the brain.

So back to the theme of this chapter. How does the hippocampus fit into this picture? As with face memory, smaller holes in the hippocampus do not seem to do much harm to name recognition, especially of names learned long ago. Patients with mild damage to the hippocampus can effortlessly come up with the last few letters when asked to complete names of famous people, such as Alfred Hitchc*** or Albert Eins****. Those who have lost all of the hippocampus together with its neighbouring structures have no clue who Alfred Hitchcock and Albert Einstein are.

Mapping Space

Space isn't remote at all. It's only an hour's drive if your car could go straight upwards. *Fred Hoyle*

One facet of the hippocampus's role in memory that everyone seems to accept is its special function in spatial learning. Finding the place where we parked the car, remembering where we left a key, flexible use of a sketch of directions to a friend's house, or imagining where a piano is located in a room, depend on our ability to create and remember mental maps of the environment. The striking feature of such mental maps is their flexibility. They can be used to guide us from any particular place to any other. If, for example, one path to our house is blocked because of road works (a frustrating experience that most of us are familiar with), another can be easily found and followed.

The ability of many animals to find their way back to their home territory over large distances also appears to be based on some type of mapping system. Perhaps the most fascinating example is the ability of many species of birds to migrate thousands of kilometres each year to reach their breeding places. The heroic effort of one of them is particularly worth mentioning. The Arctic tern appears to spend fourteen weeks of the year in its Arctic home, a bit longer in its Antarctic home, and the rest of the year in making the 35,000-kilometre round-trip flight between the two. I wonder how many free 'air miles' this bird could accumulate during its entire life if frequent-flyer services were available for birds!

To test the piloting talents of migratory birds, researchers captured them and then transported them to a position that required the birds, when released again, to change course by ninety degrees to reach their destination.[23] Interestingly, naive birds continued to fly in the same direction in which they had originally been headed and so missed their destination, while experienced birds that had made the trip before corrected for the distance they had been displaced and eventually achieved their goal. This happens because the naive birds use compass steering, which points them in a constant compass direction, whereas the experienced 'pilots' use true navigation by following a mental map, which points them towards a specific goal regardless of the original starting place and the direction necessary to achieve the goal. These are the pilot skills that we count on when we make a stop in Chicago on the way from New York to Los Angeles.

To study spatial capacity in animals in the laboratories rather than in their natural environments, psychologists have turned to white rats. They have invented a variety of spatial mazes – architectural constructions of various sizes, shapes and textures, in which different responses are required in different parts of space, as well as in different segments of time (for example, 'turn second left at this point').

Running their rats in mazes, scientists began to ask how maze habits are acquired and how they are maintained. What kind of information is essential and what is not? Is it what the rats see, hear or feel that helps them to orient themselves in the maze, to learn about space? Initial experiments were misinterpreted to suggest that mazes are learned as a chain of simple habitual movements, called stimulus–response behaviour, leading automatically to the goal. An example of stimulus–response behaviour would be to follow route instructions: keep forward for a kilometre...when you see a traffic light (stimulus) turn immediately right (response), keep going until a crossroads (stimulus), turn left (response). But subsequent research demonstrated that complex mazes could not be learned solely on the basis of stimulus and response. It became clear that maze habits were easily disrupted by simply rotating the maze relative to external visual cues in the environment (a clock, a poster or a shelf on the walls of an experimental room became favourite extra-maze cues in these experiments). A simple analogy of such habit disruption would be if one day we came into our living-room and found that our old armchair, which used to be located in the north-west corner, had been replaced in the south-east side of the room between the computer desk and the bookshelves. Although the armchair had been displaced, we would find ourselves, at least once, going towards its previous location.

Studying white rats in the fancifully named sunburst maze

(reminiscent of a child's drawing of the sun), the psychologist Edward Tolman noticed that they learn classic detour behaviour. That is, once rats had mastered the route from point A along the path BCDEF to the goal G, they would make a short cut from A to G if such a choice was available. Making short cuts, rather than making a particular sequence of responses (ABCDEFG), allows us to catch a bus at the last moment, or a friend who is about to leave the office. Similarly, clever rats who learn a *place* rather than just a simple association of movements catch food faster than their dull companions who choose do the opposite. But the benefits of dedicated 'place-learners' seem to work only if relatively varied surroundings are available with distinctive observational cues. When a plain environment is used, the superiority of the 'place-learners' disappears. In a boringly plain environment, such as in complete darkness, it becomes more efficient and safe to use stimulus–response strategies that involve, say, 'ten steps forward, turn right'.

After training rats for a few years, Tolman proposed that the spatial abilities of animals rest on the construction of internal maps, which represent the spatial relationships between various features of the environment:

> We believe that in the course of learning something like a field map of the environment gets established in the rat's brain... and it is this tentative map, indicating routes and paths and environmental relationships, which finally determines what responses, if any, the animal will finally release.[24]

All this seems to make good sense. But how and where might such mental maps be formed? Once again, H.M.'s case comes to mind, where the spatial memory deficit reflected an absent hippocampus. Scientists in many laboratories throughout the world consequently found themselves engaged in the study of memory in animals after surgical removal of the hippocampus. A large army of white rats missing their hippocampus were soon produced to participate in maze competitions. At this point, I shall take an example from my own research.

In 1977, I was studying for my undergraduate diploma thesis at the Bcritashvili Institute of Physiology at Tbilisi in Georgia. I was already an 'experienced scientist', having worked for a while on memory in monkeys in the primate behaviour laboratory. Although I was 'teaching' monkeys by myself, as a student I was not allowed to perform brain surgery on our closest relatives, apes. For my thesis, I needed something that could be done slightly faster, more independently and that would give me an opportunity to master my neurosurgical skills.

One day Olga Vinogradova, a Russian professor who was one of the pioneers of studies of single neurons in the hippocampus in awake animals, came to Tbilisi from Moscow to give a seminar. She gave an impressive talk on how memory is stored in the hippocampus and how single neurons respond to place learning. I thought that perhaps the topic of the hippocampus and spatial learning is what I should be pursuing. Temuri Naneishvili, an enthusiastic senior scientist in the lab, agreed to supervise me. We had everything on hand to test spatial memory: rats, a stereotaxic apparatus (a device to perform the brain surgery) and a T-shaped maze – a three-armed construction in which one arm serves as the start, another as the goal (providing food or water), while the third arm is empty. I fixed a peacefully sleepy, anaesthetized rat into a surgical machine, implanted thin wire electrodes into both sides of the brain, and sent a brief electric pulse through the hippocampus to destroy its back portion. The rats were then tested for their ability to solve a puzzle in the T-maze:

that is, a hungry rat had to remember to alternate its visits between arms to be rewarded by a piece of fruit. The hippocampus-less animals could cope with the task relatively well. However, when I introduced a brief pause between runs, they seemed to lose track of places previously visited. The longer the pause, the more deficit in memory was evident in the animals with a damaged hippocampus. The hippocampus, somehow, seemed important for converting fragile short-term memory into more stable, long-term storage in this spatial memory task. I put the data together to form my diploma thesis.

More and more, in different labs around the world, the hippocampus-damaged rats failed races on the spatial mazes. By the end of the 1970s T-mazes were extended and reshaped into designs with eight, twelve or sixteen arms, called radial mazes. Radial mazes allowed David Olton and others to study *working memory* in rats. This term was first introduced by a leading British psychologist, Alan Baddeley, who has devoted his academic career to studying working memory and cognition in humans.[25] Working memory is a component of short-term memory, which is 'on-line' for a few seconds and which allows us to hold in mind a telephone number long enough to order a pizza or to call a taxi. Similarly, working memory allows an animal to remember which arm has been visited and food collected from and which hasn't, so that it can make a proper decision where to go on the next trial. Olton found that rats without their hippocampus had problems in retaining such 'on-line' information. To the rats' own disappointment, they were repeatedly returning to the previously visited arms and finding nothing but empty food cups.

However, all these observations were at best only suggestive that mental maps are formed in the hippocampus. In

1978, John O'Keefe and Lynn Nadel, at University College, London, published the landmark book *The Hippocampus as a Cognitive Map*. O'Keefe and Nadel postulated that the hippocampus is well suited, both structurally and functionally, to act as a cognitive map, and is therefore crucial to memory when people or animals must remember the spatial locations of objects and events. Let us briefly consider one of the key experiments that led to such a conclusion.

O'Keefe and Nadel implanted electrodes into the hippocampus of rats and allowed the animals to run in a T-maze. They reasoned that if external cues are important for animals, just as they are for us, to create cognitive maps, then it is necessary to have the maze in an environment in which the external cues are controlled. They surrounded the maze by a set of black curtains with different cues such as a light bulb on the first wall, a poster on the second, a buzzer on the third and a fan on the fourth. The researchers designed the experiment so that the location of the goal arm of the T-maze and the four cues maintained the same spatial relationship to each other. However, during this creative and long-lasting experiment they made several modifications: they varied the spatial relation of the cues and the goal relative to the external world; changed the sequence of the arms (e.g. a start arm would become a goal); removed one or two cues, and so on. While the hungry rats were searching for the food in the maze, O'Keefe and Nadel recorded electrical responses from the neurons in the hippocampus. What they found was, indeed, amazing.

It appeared that some cells in the hippocampus, called *displace units*, are concerned only about activities in which the animal is involved, independent of where the activities take place in the environment. Other cells, *place cells*, do not care much about what activities the animal is engaged in, whether it is eating, grooming or staying still. What they seem to be exclusively affected by is the *location* of the animal in the environment. So these cells become active only when the animal navigates through a particular place in the environment. Place cells retain their recognition abilities after the removal of any single cue; but if two cues are removed or replaced, the activity of the place cell begins to modify as if the cell signals a change in the surroundings – *something is wrong here.* Perhaps such signals help us to recognize an old square when we see it after many years, even though a statue and a house that we remember might no longer be there.

O'Keefe and Nadel argued that all the behavioural changes that follow damage of the hippocampus could be explained by the loss of the ability to form mental maps. The importance of O'Keefe and Nadel's theory is extraordinary. It was the first comprehensive theory of the function of the hippocampus (although when I recently told this to John O'Keefe, he just modestly smiled and named a few others, but I did not change my mind). What is more, it contributed to the conceptual shift amongst psychologists away from the crudities of simple associationism towards an understanding of animals as thinking organisms more like humans.

Chapter 4

Almond's Fears and Emotions: The Amygdala and Remembering

Fear is not an unknown emotion to us. Neil Armstrong

In Washington Heights, until recently New York's most murderous community and America's largest wholesale cocaine market (just a few blocks from where I work), the fear still lives on.

In 1991, there were 119 killings. So far this year, the body count stands at just five. 'Business is slow now,' comments the manager of the Rivera Funeral Home on St Nicholas Avenue. 'I do not remember the last homicide we had.'[1] The trauma surgery room at Columbia Presbyterian Medical Center, the district's only hospital, where gunshot victims once rolled in on gurneys almost nightly, is now empty most nights.

Slowly, after more than fifteen years living in a war zone, people who previously would only leave their apartments in a hurry, have begun to emerge from their bunkers into the plain light of day. They now sit on a stoop, chat with a neighbour next door, or teach children how to ride a bike. New stores are opening without shields of bulletproof glass over the counters.

And yet, at every step toward normal life, the fearful memories and memories of fear seem to get in the way. Bodily trauma may be in decline, but emotional trauma is another

story. The problem here is that people have learned that they
can be harmed, and they have to watch out. Indeed, once a
person believes that a place is dangerous and threatening, it is
difficult to change this view. Not surprisingly, lessons
learned painfully are not quickly forgotten. 'I've got to get
over my fear. It controls you. It does not allow you to be. It
makes you feel like a prisoner when you have not committed
a crime,' commented Ms Pena, who has witnessed a number
of murders while growing up in the neighbourhood, about her
fears.[2] Although life is much safer there these days, the
houses, backyards and stores have all become negative emotional cues for her because of their association with
dangerous and unpleasant events.

What I have just described is called conditioned fear. To be
precise, it is conditioned *contextual* fear. It transfers meaningless stimuli into meaningful cues and binds them into one
meaningful context. It is then this particular context that
signals potentially dangerous situations. One doesn't have to
live in Washington Heights to experience fear conditioning. If
you were mugged when you visited your friend's house in
Gower Street in London, you would probably be scared every
time you visited it again. If a dog bites you while you are travelling in France, it is likely that you will feel fear afterwards
every time you hear a barking dog. If you happen to have an
abusive boss or a partner, then seeing his or her face, or even
hearing his or her voice, may cause your palms to sweat and
your heart to race (although in the latter case you might also
experience feelings of disgust or anger).

Most of our knowledge about how the brain links memory
and emotion has been gained through the study of fear conditioning in laboratory research. In a typical experiment, the
subject, a rat or a mouse for example, hears a sound that is
paired with a brief, mild electric shock to its feet. After a few

such pairings an animal responds fearfully to the sound whenever it hears it, even in the absence of the shock. This is called 'cued conditioning'. The animal will also show fear of the place where it was shocked – context conditioning. The behavioural and physiological manifestations of such responses are typical of any threatening situation: the animal startles, and its autonomic responses – blood pressure, breathing and heart rate – increase. It crouches and freezes. This is extraordinarily similar to what happens to humans when they experience fear, as vividly described by Charles Darwin:

> The frightened man at first stands like a statue, motionless or breathless, or crouches down as if instinctively to escape observation. The heart beats quickly and violently, so that it palpitates or knocks against the ribs.[3]

However, on some occasions, as a result of conditioning, an animal might flee if there is a way to escape; or it might show an aggressive response and attack a threatening animal. For example, if a mouse is placed with a rat during conditioning, the rat might attack the mouse (it certainly would be unwise for the mouse to try to attack the rat).

The first fear conditioning experiment was performed in Vladimir Bekhterev's laboratory, in Petrograd (now St Petersburg) at the beginning of the twentieth century. Bekhterev and his colleagues did their initial experiments on volunteer male subjects.[4] The subject was asked to sit in a chair, in an experimental room, and to rest one foot on a pedal connected to a shock generator (Figure 5). At a certain time, the researchers delivered sounds of a violin into the experimental room. The musical sounds alone would not cause any harm or fear.[5] However, the experiment was designed so that

Figure 5 Bekhterev's fear-conditioning experiment

every time the music was in the air, the patient received a brief mild shock to his bare foot. The Russian scientists found that relatively few such pairings were enough for the subject to learn to withdraw his foot whenever he heard the sounds of the violin. Similar experiments were performed on dogs (dogs of course never volunteered for such experiments).

Conditioned fear is one variation of 'classical' conditioning – the procedure discovered by the Nobel prizewinner Ivan Pavlov around the turn of the last century.[6] In Pavlov's most famous experiment, a bell was rung just before a piece of juicy meat was delivered to a dog's mouth. At first, the dog did not salivate until it got the meat. After the relationship between the bell and the meat had been established (the association in the brain between these events), it salivated at the sound of the bell. Finally, Pavlov found that the dog would continue responding to the bell even if it was not followed by meat – at least for a while. Eventually, the dog would stop salivating at the sound of the bell unless meat was offered periodically. Pavlov called the bell a conditioned stimulus, the meat an unconditioned stimulus, and the animal's responses to the sound of the bell conditioned responses. Applying this terminology to the experiment described above, the sound was a conditioned stimulus, the foot shock was an unconditioned stimulus, and the withdraw or freeze reaction was a conditioned response.

It is essential for animals to learn to fear dangerous situations, and they are generally able to do so rapidly. Often a single pairing of the conditioned and unconditioned stimulus is enough for strong conditioned fear to be formed. This makes perfect evolutionary sense, because in the wild animals rarely have the luxury of trial-and-error learning. Once an encounter with a predator has been survived, memory of this experience can be used in a similar situation next time. If a mouse barely escapes a cat's teeth while searching for a piece of cheese in a kitchen, it will approach the same place with trepidation next time, searching the surroundings for any possible clue that might signal the existence of a cat near by.

Conditioned fear is also long-lasting. Mice, for example, will show clear signs of fear conditioning (e.g. freezing) even three months after a single pairing of conditioned and unconditioned stimulus. The passing of time is not enough to forget a bitter experience. Nonetheless, repeated exposures to a conditioned stimulus without an unconditioned stimulus will finally diminish the fear response. This is called 'extinction'. If our hungry mouse has no other place to search for food and it runs to a kitchen again and again without encountering a cat, it will eventually act as if it never met a cat there.

Extinction does not mean the complete elimination of the relationship between the conditioned and the unconditioned stimulus. Memory for a conditioned stimulus once associated with a danger does not disappear entirely. Once extinguished, the responses might re-appear – Pavlov called this 'spontaneous recovery' – or the responses might be reinstated when the animals are exposed to stressful events. These animal findings extend beyond the laboratory and fit well with observations on human pathological fears such as phobias.[7] Often, as a result of treatment, it seems as if a patient is capable of keeping a phobia under control. And yet an unrelated stressful or traumatic event can then be the cause for the reinstatement of the pathological fear. Similarly to extinction, treatment does not erase the memory that ties the fear reaction to the trigger stimuli, but simply prevents the stimuli from inducing the fear response.[8] Perhaps similar processes happen in the brain when we 'forgive but can't forget'.

The longevity of conditioned fear has its pros and cons. Certainly, it is extremely important to maintain memories of events and situations that have been associated with danger in the past. However, because such memories are often formed in traumatic situations – as we have already seen with Ms Pena – they may interfere with everyday life. I'll say more about traumatic memory later in this chapter. But here I want to mention another interesting facet of conditioned fear: namely, that fear conditioning can occur without conscious awareness of the conditioned stimulus and its relation to the unconditioned stimulus. One source of evidence for this comes from human studies performed by Arne Ohman and co-workers at the Karolinska Hospital, Stockholm. These researchers tested some eight hundred subjects with so-called 'backward masking' – the procedure believed to allow the conditioned stimulus to enter the brain but not to enter the consciousness.[9] The second source of evidence is less direct but seems to me even more convincing. Fear conditioning can be studied – at least as a defensive response to the neutral conditioned stimulus – in species as different as flies and mice, snails and cats, worms and dogs, frogs and chicks, lizards and rats, fish and people. 'I doubt that all of these animals consciously experience fear in the presence of a conditioned stimulus that predicts danger,' says Joseph LeDoux, a neuroscientist at New York University who devoted most of his career to the study of neural mechanisms of fear and memory, and I agree with him.[10]

What neural circuits and cellular mechanisms are critical to fear memories? The remarkable fact is that within mammals the behavioural expression of fear conditioning and the brain structures involved in fear responses are very similar. The similarities are even more striking when the discussion comes down to molecules and genes – here we appear to be close relatives to species as primitive as flies and snails.

The Seat of All Fears

Nothing in life is to be feared. It is only to be understood. *Marie Curie*

The amygdala, an almond-shaped complex of tiny interconnected structures buried in the depths of the temporal lobe next to the hippocampus, is the master of emotional matters. Just like the hippocampus, there are two amygdalas, one on each side of the brain. The hippocampus and the amygdala were the two key structures of the primitive 'nose brain' that gave rise to the neocortex – the folded layer that grew massive in human evolution and is the seat of thought, reason and intellect. The hippocampus, as we have already seen, plays a key role in our ability to learn and remember ongoing events; the amygdala is specialized for emotional memory. The amygdala is a key player in emotional learning because of its central location between input and output stations. Each route that leads to the amygdala – sensory thalamus, sensory cortex and hippocampus – carries unique information to the organ. The amygdala in turn sends signals to virtually every other part of the brain, including the decision-making centre of the frontal lobe – the prefrontal cortex (*see* Figure 3).

The importance of the amygdala in emotion was first suggested by the pioneering findings of Heinrich Klüver and Paul Bucy in 1937, and Lawrence Weiskrantz in 1956.[11] Working with monkeys, these researchers discovered that if the amygdala was removed from the rest of the brain, the behaviour of these primates became aberrant: they lost their terror of previously feared objects (such as snakes or people) that still frightened their normal companions; repeatedly failed to avoid noxious stimuli; attempted to copulate with members of different species; and tried to eat inappropriate objects such as rocks, faeces or even live rats. Klüver and Bucy referred to this collection of symptoms as 'psychic blindness', by which they meant that even though the animals retained perfectly good visual acuity and motor function, they were blind to the emotional importance of events. Such bizarre behaviour became known as the Klüver–Bucy syndrome. Later studies revealed that this phenomenon extends beyond the laboratory.

Life without an amygdala is life without feelings. One young man whose amygdala had been surgically removed to reduce severe seizures became completely indifferent to people, spending time by doing nothing but sitting in isolation, with no human contacts.[12] He no longer recognized his close friends, relatives or even his mother, and remained nonchalant in the face of their sadness at his impassivity. He seemed to have lost all his abilities to recognize feelings, or the emotional significance of the events happening around him. No memories could provoke tears of sorrow or smiles of happiness; no stories could frighten him. The 'storehouse' of his emotional memory seemed lost forever.

People who have had their amygdala removed or damaged lose the desire to cooperate or compete, and no longer have the proper sense of their social status. They lack the ability to detect fear, sadness, disgust or rage. The memories related to fear seem to suffer the most. A study by Antonio Damasio's team has specifically linked the amygdala with recognition of fear.[13] They examined nineteen patients: one, a thirty-year-old woman known as S.M., had nearly complete atrophy of both amygdalas as a result of a rare genetic disease, known as Urbach–Weithe disease; six subjects had damage restricted to only one amygdala; and the remaining twelve patients, the 'control' group, had lesions in other parts of the brain, but retained intact amygdalas. Subjects were shown slides of human facial expressions indicating fear, anger, happiness and so on. They were asked to identify what kind of emotions the faces expressed and to judge the intensity of the emotional expressions (e.g. 'How angry does this person look?'). These experiments clearly demonstrated that if both sides of the amygdala are damaged, the processing of fearful facial expressions is totally lost. The subject S.M. commented that she simply 'did not know what an afraid face would look like'. Indeed, being very proficient at drawing, she was able to produce without difficulty pictures of all facial expressions except fear.

Damage to the amygdala not only blunts recognition of fear, but also impairs judgement of the intensity of expressions such as surprise, anger or disgust. In particular, the amygdala is important in the social judgement of faces classified as unapproachable and untrustworthy. These findings clearly indicate the crucial role of the amygdala in recognition both of the basic emotion of fear and of many of the nuances of the different emotions that the human face is capable of signalling. The amygdala therefore appears to be a key player in the neural systems subserving social cognition, because fine-tuned recognition of the emotions signalled by faces is essential for successful behaviour in our complicated world.

Studies of patients with damaged amygdalas have offered additional insights into its function. In 1997, a group of British scientists led by Andrew Young described a patient (D.R.) whose amygdala had been surgically removed to relieve severe seizures.[14] Like Damasio's patients, D.R. was unable to recall or recognize facial expressions of fear, even though she had no problem identifying familiar faces. She also had impaired recognition of the vocal expressions of emotion, despite having perfect hearing. Even more striking, as was the case for facial expressions, it was recognition of fear and anger that was most severely affected in the auditory domain. In fact, findings of impaired processing of social signals from the voice should not come as a great surprise: even though the amygdala contains many cells sensitive to faces, it also receives inputs from the other senses and is therefore in a perfect position to be involved in general judgement of danger and the recognition of fear.

The view that the amygdala is involved in emotionally related memory is strongly supported by fear conditioning experiments. In the cued conditioning experiment I described earlier, the rats will not learn to fear the sound of the tone if their amygdala is damaged. Even if the animals receive a few pairings of conditioned and unconditioned stimulus, the next time they hear the same sound they show no signs of fear. The experiments by Joseph LeDoux and co-workers have demonstrated that to produce such impairment it is enough to inactivate a tiny single structure within the amygdala, known as the lateral nucleus. However, one needs to inactivate more of the central part of the amygdala to produce a deficit in contextual conditioning. Contextual conditioning is also wiped out by lesions of the hippocampus, whereas cued conditioning is not.

Searching for neural substrates of emotional conditioning in humans, Damasio's team investigated S.M., along with two other patients – one with selective damage to both sides of the hippocampus, and the other with damage to both amygdala and the hippocampus – for their ability to learn fear conditioning.[15] The basic design of the experiment was as follows: the subjects were presented with colour slides – red, blue, green or yellow – and the blue slide was accompanied by a startlingly loud sound of a boat horn. This noxious noise produced an emotional arousal, which was easily detectable as an increase in the electrical conductivity of the skin. A few minutes after completion of the conditioning procedure, the participants were tested for their explicit memory of what happened during the experiment with questions such as, 'How many different colours did you see?', 'What are the names of these colours?' and 'What was the colour that was followed by the horn?' After a few pairings of the blue slide with the unpleasant sound, the normal subjects were emotionally conditioned: every time the blue slide was shown alone, their skin conductance increased. The patient with the damage restricted to the hippocampus, as expected from previous findings in hippocampus-damaged humans, showed normal emotional conditioning but remembered little of what was going on during the conditioning episode. So what the subjects could not consciously remember – whether they feared blue or red – was easily uncovered by the famous lie-detector test. In contrast, S.M., whose amygdala was damaged but whose hippocampus was intact, remembered what had happened during the conditioning episode, but showed no signs of emotional conditioning. And the third patient, with damage to both structures, despite his above-average intellectual abilities, had no conscious or emotional awareness of what had happened: he neither recalled the experiment nor showed any evidence of emotional conditioning. The importance of these extraordinary findings is two-fold. First, they clearly demonstrate that the amygdala is indispensable for fear conditioning. Second, they illustrate the double dissociation between the emotional (implicit) and declarative (explicit) aspects of memory.

There is one final point I want to make. Although the weight of evidence strongly indicates that the amygdala is important for learning and remembering fears, one should keep in mind that it is not the only learning centre. The establishment of memories depends on the working of the entire brain network, not just of one component. 'Memory is like a piece of music – it has lots of different parts that come together to create the whole,' writes Marcus Raichle.

Emergency Route

Recent research has unveiled some important clues about how the amygdala can take control over what we fear, while the rational brain, the cortex, is still thinking what to do. As I already mentioned, the brain's architecture is arranged so that the amygdala is perfectly placed to receive inputs from many other structures in the brain and at the same time send outputs to them. It therefore acts something like a 999 service where the operators are ready to receive emergency calls and send them out immediately where necessary (although the amygdala never responds with the ridiculous 'Emergency, please hold'). When there is danger or fear, the amygdala transmits urgent signals to every major structure in the brain: it triggers the production of the body's 'flight or fight' hormones, fixes the face in a fearful expression, mobilizes the centres for movement, and increases blood flow to the muscles.

In an extensive series of fear conditioning experiments on rats, LeDoux revealed how the organization of the brain gives the amygdala a privileged role in quickly detecting the emotional significance of threatening information. LeDoux's experimental scheme involved the pairing of a sound with a mild electric shock as described above. 'My approach was to let the natural flow of information through the brain be my guide,' says LeDoux, and he started at the beginning: that is, where the sound-conditioned stimulus enters the brain. Obviously, reasoned LeDoux, destroying the ears would be unwise, because a deaf rat would not be able to learn anything about a sound. So instead he began by damaging the next parts of the auditory pathway: the auditory cortex (which is located in humans on the upper surface of the temporal lobe), and the auditory thalamus (which comprises a pair of brain structures located close to the midline of the brain just below the ears). LeDoux found that only lesions of the auditory thalamus prevented fear conditioning. So he decided to investigate relay stations further down in the brain. Indeed, the destruction of the next lower auditory station – the auditory midbrain – had a similar impairing effect. This was puzzling for the following reason.

The traditional view in neuroscience had been that the ears (or other sensory organs) transmit signals to the thalamus, and from there to sensory processing areas of the cortex – the culmination of a sequence of neural steps starting (in this case) in the ear. In the cortex, the signals are put together and sorted for meaning so that the brain recognizes what each stimulus is and what its presence means. But the lesions of the auditory cortex in LeDoux's experiments did not affect fear conditioning: a rat remembered the scary sound and froze when it heard it again. Where else, then – LeDoux wondered – was the auditory stimulus travelling and taking its emotional message after leaving the thalamus, if not to the cortex? He soon discovered a smaller bundle of neurons that originate in the sensory thalamus and lead directly from the thalamus to the amygdala. It is this 'short cut' that allows the amygdala to receive direct input from the senses and initiate the 'flight or fight' responses while the cortex is still making its decision.

Threatening and dangerous events require immediate attention and action. The direct pathways from thalamus to the amygdala provide an unrefined perception of the external world, but because they involve only one neural link, they are very fast. In contrast, pathways from the cortex offer detailed and accurate representations of external events, but these pathways, which run from the thalamus to the sensory cortex and then to the amygdala, involve several neural links. This adds time, and so does thinking, whereas reaction to danger often requires a rapid response.

Saving time may be the reason for an additional, direct route for emotional learning. A normally functioning amygdala can trigger an emotional response via this emergency route even as a parallel neuronal circuit is activated between the amygdala and cortex. The cortex is not needed to establish simple fear conditioning; it comes into action only when it is necessary to interpret more complex stimuli explicitly, whereas the amygdala is capable of perceiving, remembering and orchestrating fear independently of explicit memory of the conditioning episode. There is, however, more to say about the amygdala: an activated amygdala can also influence or modulate explicit memory for emotionally significant events, thereby promoting accurate explicit memory for these events. Let's briefly consider how the amygdala might do so.

Modulatory Route

Jim McGaugh at the University of California at Irvine has long been concerned with the modulatory role of the amygdala in memory storage.[16] McGaugh's team found that if animals are given a shot of noradrenaline (a stress-related hormone, also known as norepinephrine, that is released during emotional states of fear or happiness) immediately after the learning experience, their memory for the learning situation is improved (in popular terminology, the hormone acts as a 'smart' drug). McGaugh's group also demonstrated that mild electrical stimulation of the amygdala immediately after an animal has learned something new could enhance subsequent memory for the task. This effect is also attributed to noradrenaline because the beneficial effects of electrical stimulation of the amygdala disappear if the adrenal medulla (which produces noradrenaline) is removed. To reinforce the view of the amygdala's modulatory role in memory storage, McGaugh's group turned to lesion techniques and removed the amygdala from rats' brains. Without the amygdala, the memory-improving effects of the hormones disappeared. These findings suggest that if stress hormones are released naturally in an emotionally significant situation, the experience will be remembered especially well (it is, however, also known that excessive arousal can have an opposite, memory-impairing effect). Because emotional arousal results in the release of stress hormones, it is likely that the explicit memory for emotional events would be stronger than explicit memory for non-emotional events. If so, then the administration of drugs that interfere with stress-release hormones should prevent the usual beneficial effects of emotional arousal on memory. The Californian scientists soon provided evidence for this.

In an ingeniously designed experiment, McGaugh and Larry Cahill tested the memory of two groups of volunteer subjects.[17] One group was given a simple story to read in which a little boy rides a bicycle, goes home, from where his mother drives him to the hospital to pick up his father, who works there as a doctor. Another group was given a similar story to read, but with additional emotional meaning: a boy rides a bicycle, is hit by a car and rushed to the hospital where his father works as a doctor. Immediately after reading the stories, half of the experimental volunteers in each group were given a placebo pill, and the other half were given propranolol, a drug that blocks the effects of noradrenaline. After this all participants were asked to recall the story as well as they could. The placebo subjects remembered the emotionally arousing story more accurately than the non-emotional one, whereas the group receiving the drug did not demonstrate such an arousal benefit – they recalled the emotional and non-emotional stories to a similar extent. These findings indicate that blocking the action of stress-related hormones interferes with the memory-facilitating effects of emotional arousal. Similar results were observed when emotionally arousing and emotionally neutral slides were used instead of stories. These remarkable findings may have some important practical implications. It is possible that the blocking of excessive stress-released hormones after some traumatic events might help people to cope with fear and anguish later.

Memory storage is also influenced by other hormonal and neuromodulatory systems. Fear memories are weakened, for example, by the release of naturally occurring morphine-like molecules called opioids. These compounds are our natural painkillers: athletes, people with schizophrenia and people who meditate, all of whom are less sensitive to pain, produce a lot of them. A gamut of pleasant emotional states – the emotional thrill from hearing our favourite song, watching our football team winning a championship, or drinking a third glass of champagne at our birthday celebration – are almost always associated with an increase in opioid levels. These opioid molecules, however, are also produced in times of trouble and danger to protect us from pain, shock or severe stress. Perhaps their capacity to interfere with memory storage is an aspect of this protective mechanism.

Opioids became extremely fashionable in the 1980s and I was lured by their appeal. While working on my PhD thesis at the Institute of Normal Physiology in Moscow, I became interested in how these molecules affect emotional states. Fear can easily be induced by brief electrical stimulation of the front portion of the hypothalamus, a small structure located deep in both sides of the brain, which along with the amygdala is involved in the control of emotions. In rabbits, a few milliseconds of stimulation is enough to induce fear: a scared rabbit runs to a corner of the experimental box, its heart rate, breathing and blood pressure increase, and it sits with eyes shut. Conversely, when I stimulated the back portion of the hypothalamus, rabbits liked it. As they had with fear, they seemed to sense 'pleasant electricity' immediately: within a few minutes they learned to press the knob that was connected to the electric source delivering current into their brain. This is called self-stimulation. Obviously, it is difficult to establish what sort of pleasure animals experience, but both rabbits and rats will self-stimulate for hours, and seem very upset if you unplug the electricity supply.

I found that opioids, if injected into rabbits, impaired emotional responses. Similar findings were repeatedly documented in rats and humans. McGaugh suggests that such influences, like those of noradrenaline, involve the amygdala. As he observed with noradrenaline, opioid effects are blocked by destruction of the amygdala or the neuronal pathways leading to it. Furthermore, memory 'ups and downs' appeared to be due to modulation of the release of noradrenaline within the amygdala. Similarly, benzodiazepines – drugs used in humans to reduce anxiety and to aid sleep – impair memory through their influence on the amygdala.

There is, of course, more to say about other hormonal and neuromodulatory systems that might affect memory storage by influencing activity in the amygdala. It is debatable, however, whether influences of the amygdala on memory storage are due to modulation of cell-to-cell communication within the amygdala, or whether the amygdala affects remembering by modulation of the formation of memory traces in other brain regions. The most prominent advocates of the second view are McGaugh's team, while LeDoux's supporters believe that cellular changes underlying fear memory take place in the amygdala (see Chapter 6).

Moody Memory and the Millionaire

Events that we learn in one emotional state may be remembered better when we revert to the state we were in during the original experience. This is called state-dependent memory. But what do we actually mean by the term 'state'?

It can refer to any external or internal condition of our body or mind. The fundamental feature of state-dependent memory is that the closer the match between the states under which original learning and retrieval took place, the better the recall. To illustrate state-dependent memory, the psychologist Gordon Bower at Stanford University, who studies memory in humans, cites the adventures of Charlie Chaplin's little tramp in the classic film *City Lights*. Charlie saves a drunken millionaire from leaping to his death. The two then spend the evening together drinking, dancing and having fun. The next day, when sober, the millionaire does not recognize the tramp and tells his butler to throw him out of the house. Later the millionaire gets drunk again, and when he spots the tramp, he greets him as his dear friend.

Psychologists adopted the 'millionaire' experience in labs. Most of the early work on state-dependent memory involved different kinds of drugs, including stimulants such as marijuana, barbiturates and alcohol, to induce changes in emotional state. Invariably, the findings of these studies supported the existence of drug-induced state-dependent memory. By the late 1970s, in an attempt to find out how memory is influenced by emotions, scientists began to turn their attention to exploring whether or not mood states could also be important for state-dependent memory.[18] Enchanted by Charlie's experience, Bower and co-workers chose to work with happiness and sadness, in the laboratory, using college students.

There are several techniques for producing moods. Subjects might be asked to watch sad or funny movies, listen to records, read stories, or to imagine and remember a scene in which they have been ecstatically happy or painfully sad. In one particular experiment, students were asked to keep detailed diaries of their emotional ups and downs. A week

later, they were put through mood-manipulating procedures
and tested for recall of every incident from their diaries. All
matched memory to mood: happy students (those who
watched comedy) remembered more of their pleasant experiences than unpleasant incidents, whereas unhappy students
recalled more unpleasant and sad events.[19]

Psychiatrists observed one of the clearest early examples
of mood-dependent memory. Psychiatric patients with
manic-depressive mood swings were asked to generate
twenty free associations to each of two novel stimulus words,
and to reproduce them a few days later. During all this time
the clinicians monitored the patients' emotional states.
When tested, it was obvious that the greater the change in
patients' states – from mania to depression, and vice versa –
the more they forgot the target associations generated a few
days before. In another example, the more severe the
patients' depression, the longer it took the patients to recall a
pleasant incident than an unpleasant incident.

However they are created, mood effects on memory are typically small.[20] Unless the moods induced are fairly intense and
the two mood conditions are substantially different from one
another, then mood-dependent retrieval is unlikely. Effects
depend on many things; for instance, mood-dependent
retrieval is rarely observed with recognition memory tests or
strongly cued recall tests, but reliably appears when people
recall autobiographical memories in different mood states.
How might these effects be formed? Many psychologists
believe that memories are stored in associative neural networks in which each event is represented by a cluster of
descriptive components, all linked to each other (see Chapter
2). To remember an event consciously, the associative
network has to reach a certain level of activation – a threshold
– which depends on the number of components of the memory

that are activated, and how much each component contributes to the overall memory in the network. Essential aspects of a memory contribute more than things that are less essential. The more cues match between original learning and subsequent retrieval, the stronger the neural networks activated by these cues – and the more likely it is that the memory will occur.

Where Were You Then?

I really believe there are things nobody would see if I did not photograph them. *Diane Arbus*

August 1991, Moscow. I was staying in the Hotel Academicheskya, sharing a room with a young scientist, an ecologist, who was on her way back home to Novosibirsk after a few months' work in Holland. In contrast, I was on my way from my home town of Tbilisi to England to work at the Open University with Steven Rose on biochemistry and memory in young chicks.

I was woken early in the morning by an unexpected telephone call. It was a call from Novosibirsk for my room-mate. The next thing I remember is an expression of fear on her face, and her repeatedly mumbling, almost crying, 'But I want to come home, I want to come home... can I come home? How?' I looked at her, not knowing what was going on. I remember feeling concerned because of her expression of fear, but I was also surprised. What could possibly prevent her from going back home? I knew that she was going to fly that afternoon. She looked at me and told me the news.

In Novosibirsk, which is four hours ahead of Moscow, people had already learned that Mikhail Gorbachev had been arrested in his dacha in the Crimea. They knew there was a coup. At that moment, the stunning news sounded to me like the end of democratic reform and the beginning of bloodshed. I had the feeling that doors were closed and windows were shut. I remember fear, a very strong fear of being three thousand kilometres away from my home, separated from my son, who was then studying in Norway, and my husband and my mother, who were in Tbilisi. Should I go back to Tbilisi? Should I? Could I? Or should I go to England, abroad, away from this country? Could I? When would I see my family? Would I? All these vital questions were processed within only a few milliseconds in my brain, but an image of the moment when I first heard the news, an image of that woman sitting in her bed with a telephone, saying, 'I want to come home!' has remained fixed in my mind for over ten years.

We turned on the television and heard the news. At the same time – at least that's how I remember it – I heard a loud noise outside. I knew that noise from other occasions. I looked through the window...the tanks were filling up the streets of Moscow. For me, and for many of us 'ex-Soviets', the memory of that August morning in 1991 seems frozen in photographic form.

Many of you would probably now claim to recall in vivid detail, and with great confidence, where you were and what you were doing when you first learned about the death of Diana, Princess of Wales, or about the tragic explosion of the space shuttle *Challenger*. If so, then you may have experienced what has been coined a 'flashbulb' memory. Almost all of us have at least some flashbulb memories. Some of them are triggered by events common to many people because they have national or international importance (the assassination of President Kennedy, or the killing of John Lennon), while others are of a strictly personal nature (the death of a friend or relative, a serious accident, or the winning of a Nobel prize).

A flashbulb memory is thought to be an unusually detailed, vivid recollection of a surprising, important and emotionally arousing event. In 1977 the psychologists Roger Brown and James Kulik suggested that a novel and shocking event triggers a special neural mechanism, which they referred to as *Now Print*.[21] Just like a camera's flashbulb, the *Now Print* mechanism preserves or 'freezes' into permanent memory an astonishing number of details about the circumstances that occurred at the moment we first learned of the shocking event.

Brown and Kulik interviewed forty white and forty black Americans about their recollections of shocking public events such as the assassinations of President Kennedy, Martin Luther King, Malcolm X and Robert Kennedy. The informants were given credit for a flashbulb memory whenever they answered 'yes' to the question, 'Do you recall the circumstances in which you first heard...?' and whenever they could describe in detail how they learned about it, whom they were with, where they were or how they felt at the time. Ninety-nine per cent of the informants reported flashbulb memories of the shooting of President Kennedy. Brown and Kulik attributed this to the unusual importance of this event for the entire US population. In contrast, less than fifty per cent of both whites and blacks possessed flashbulb memories of Robert Kennedy's assassination. Seventy-five per cent of blacks but only thirty-two per cent of whites showed flashbulb memories of King's assassination. The psychologists proposed that the degree of the 'consequentiality' of the dramatic event determines whether the *Now Print* mechanism is activated and the brain's flashbulb pops. They also assumed that the circumstances surrounding the shocking event would be accurate and largely immune to forgetting, in part because of frequent rehearsal of the details of the story.

The assumption that flashbulb memories are in some way special is intuitively compelling, and fits well with the subjective experiences of many of us who have experienced them. But how accurate is our account of flashbulb memories? Are they established and maintained in a different way from more 'ordinary' memories? Is the event somehow engraved permanently in our minds in its original form like a photograph that indiscriminately preserves the scene?

A photograph retains everything within its scope. Our flashbulb memories do not. For instance, when I say, 'I remember my hotel neighbour sitting in her bed with a telephone,' I cannot really say whether she was sitting under the blanket or over it, whether she was holding the telephone in her left or right hand, or what sort of nightdress she was wearing. All these would be preserved in a real photograph, of course. Perhaps I remembered all these details for a day or two, but then forgot them, or perhaps I paid no attention to them at all. After all, why would all that matter? What is interesting, however, is that although in my case it was important *where I was* when I learned about the news (in the centre of events, away from my family and home), what difference does it make for most people *where they were* when they heard about the *Challenger* explosion, or who told them the news? None, really. Why, then, do people seem to remember such things? Events like these, for sure, will be pondered, discussed and re-described on subsequent occasions. 'Why shouldn't we suppose that their persistence is due to the frequent reconsideration they receive?' suggested the Cornell University psychologist Ulric Neisser.[22] In fact, Neisser believes that memories become flashbulbs primarily through the significance attached to them afterwards. If so, then such memories might be inaccurate.

Indeed, an example of the fallibility of flashbulb memories

was demonstrated by the perceptive work of Ulric Neisser and Nicole Harsch. Suspecting that the *Challenger* explosion had all the features for becoming a flashbulb memory, they interviewed 106 college students less than twenty-four hours after the event and then again two-and-half years later. After this long interval, students had substantially forgotten their original descriptions. What is remarkable, however, is that many students were very confident that their now false recollections were correct. The forgetfulness, it seems to me, could easily be explained by the fact that the *Challenger* disaster did not have much of the 'consequentiality' for students in the sense that it was originally defined by Brown and Kulik (when rating 'consequentiality' Brown and Kulik instructed students to ask themselves, 'What consequences for my life, both direct and indirect, has this event had?'). Let's consider some other examples.

In 1990, the British psychologist Martin Conway and his colleagues interviewed over three hundred British and American college students within two weeks of the unexpected resignation of the prime minister, Margaret Thatcher.[23] A year later, the investigators questioned the students again. British students accurately recalled how they learned of the news, whereas American students had largely forgotten (in fact, I'm surprised that they even noticed this event). Here is another example, reported by Neisser and his colleagues which, I think, is not surprising at all. Californians who were affected by the 1989 earthquake in San Francisco retained extremely accurate memories when tested several years later, whereas people from Atlanta, who had only heard about the tragic event on the news, did not. On the one hand, this evidence seems to support the view of Brown and Kulik that personal significance of a flashbulb event – 'consequentiality' – has a crucial role in the immunity of the memory for the event. On the other hand, it strengthens Neisser's idea about the significance attached to flashbulb memories after the event. It is very likely that Conway's British students discussed how they heard the news with their friends over a pint of beer later that day, and perhaps even over the following couple of days, whereas the American students did not.

I can supply another example from my own experience, which I believe constitutes a strong flashbulb event for many people and supports the idea that flashbulb memories depend on what happens after the event rather than its consequentiality. Knowing that I would be writing this book, I wrote down a detailed account of how I learned the news of Princess Diana's tragic death. Twenty-five hours and twenty-five months later I checked my memories of the event. They were extremely accurate twenty-five hours later; they were still accurate, although less detailed, twenty-five months later. What possible consequentiality could Diana's death have for my family or me? None at all. Then why do I remember that midnight, but not the midnight before? I have to agree with Neisser that 'we remember the details of a flashbulb occasion because those details are the links between our own histories and "History".' I was alone at home waiting for my husband to come back from Massachusetts. I had serious back problems and was in a lot of pain that night…I recall being in my living-room lying on the sofa with an ice-pack under my back; I turned on the television and heard the news. A few minutes later my husband came home, and I told him the news. Thus, I rehearsed the news – that was the first 'afterwards'. Over the next few days, sick and in bed, I rehearsed the tragic event as often as I tried to watch the news.

We rehearse dramatic public events often in our minds. Sometimes we may not even do this willingly, but cannot avoid doing so because of media influence and conversations

going on around us. Frequent rehearsal and discussion probably contribute to the accuracy of our memory, but not necessarily always. In addition to the account of public events that
we all retain to some extent, we often elaborate our own
story. Our flashbulb memories are therefore sometimes inac-
curately pruned. For instance, the Danish psychologist Steen
Larsen was sure that he had heard about the 1986 assassination of the Swedish prime minister Olaf Palme on the radio
while having breakfast with his wife.[24] To his own surprise,
Larsen discovered that his wife was not even at home at that
time. Why did his wife become 'inserted' in the story? What
contributed to Larsen's varnished memory? There are several
possibilities. First, once he heard the news, he could have
imagined how he would discuss this event with his wife and
this image could have been 'inserted' into his memory as if it
were real. Second, it is likely that he discussed this event
with his wife later and that he confused his two sources of
knowledge. Such 'insertion' is also not surprising considering
that it is often routine for a married couple to have breakfast
together.

Although flashbulb memories are prone to similar sorts of
'insertions', confusions and forgetting, they still are better
remembered than memories of everyday events. The high
emotional arousal, as well as frequent rehearsal, contributes
to the vividness of our recollection. That's why I remember
what happened on 19 August 1991, but not on 19 August
1990 or 1992. Later that night, I was sitting in Steven Rose's
house in London, greatly concerned about what was going to
happen in my country, rehearsing the event over a glass of
wine by describing to Steven and his wife, Hilary, the exact
moment at which I heard the news. The next few days were
spent not only in studying the memory of chicks, but also in
strengthening my own flashbulb memory of the coup by

discussing with my British colleagues and friends where I was when I heard the news and how I'd heard about it.

Scar Tissue: Traumatic Memories

The only way to get rid of my fears is to make films about them.
Alfred Hitchcock

'An experience may be so exciting emotionally as almost to leave a scar on cerebral tissues,' wrote William James in 1890.[25] Most people, at one time or another, have experienced a traumatic event that may feel as though it has left a lifelong scar in the brain. I will never forget the horror I felt when I learned about my father's deadly disease. I also remember very well where I was and how terrible I felt when I received a telephone call informing me that the ten-year-old child of a very close friend had had a tragic accident during a skiing competition. On the positive side, I am deeply thankful that I retain many emotionally positive memories of my childhood, memories of my parents, always warm and loving; the exact moment I saw for the first time my son's face, heard him saying 'dada' (which means 'mama' in Georgian) or watched him making his first steps. Such emotional memories seem to me always fresh, always available and always accessible. 'The memory is a living thing – it too is in transit. But during its moment, all that is remembered joins, and lives – the old and the young, the past and the present, the living and the dead,' writes Eudora Welty in *One Writer's Beginnings* '...to the memory nothing is lost.'

Scientists have long been interested in the nature of memory for emotionally arousing and traumatic events. Endless wars, concentration camps, terrorist actions, criminal violence, abuse of children and women, and natural disasters, to name just a few, create a vast number of victims with extreme and unusual traumatic memories.[26] Although the causes of psychological trauma vary widely, traumatic memories have several common qualities. A traumatized person may experience intense emotion but have no clear memory of the harmful event, or may remember everything in detail but show no emotion. Sometimes traumatic memories become disconnected from their original source. A person might be in a constant state of vigilance and irritability without knowing why. This sort of fragmentation, whereby traumatic memories tear apart our system of self-protection, is a central characteristic of post-traumatic stress disorder.

Traumatic memories affect the course of normal development by their repetitive intrusion into the survivor's life. Pierre Janet, for example, described his patients with hysteria as being dominated by an *idée fixe* and lacking the capacity to harmonize the memory of overwhelming life events.[27] He believed that traumatic memories were preserved in an abnormal state, set aside from ordinary consciousness. Freud wrote about the essential pathology of the combat traumatic memories after the First World War in similar words: 'The patient, one might say, is fixated to the trauma.'[28]

Unlike normal memory which is like 'the action of telling a story', traumatic memory is repetitious, stereotyped and often wordless. This unusual quality of traumatic memories was well captured by Doris Lessing in her novel *A Small Personal Voice*, in which she described her father, a war veteran who considered himself lucky to have lost only a leg while the rest of his friends lost their lives:

> His childhood and young man's memories, kept fluid, were added to, grew, as living memories do. But his war memories were congealed in stories that he told again and again, with the same words and gestures, in stereotyped phrases... This dark

region in him, fate-ruled, where nothing was true but horror, was expressed inarticulately, in brief, bitter exclamations of rage, incredulity, betrayal.[29]

Recollections of real-life traumatic events provide important insights into emotional memory. The psychiatrist Charles Wilkinson consulted 102 victims and observers of the horrible collapse of two skywalks at the Hyatt Regency Hotel in Kansas City on 17 July 1981. The disaster killed 114 people and injured more than two hundred. A few weeks following the traumatic event, 90 per cent of the observers complained that the memories kept coming back. Most of them also experienced difficulties in remembering routine daily events, presumably, suggested Wilkinson, because they were so depressed, distracted or detached that they could not remember ongoing events normally.[30] Such profound reactions and recollections are not unique. Similar feelings are evident in the story of my Russian colleague, Anya Tiunova, who witnessed a huge explosion of an apartment block in Moscow on 10 September 1999. The blast – thought to have been planned by Chechnyan terrorists – demolished more than sixty apartments in the centre of the building, leaving a gaping nine-storey hole between the remaining two wings of the structure with nothing but 90 dead and 150 injured people between them. 'I keep remembering the horrible sound,' she told me two weeks later. 'I have images of the ruins…smoke…I am scared to have the children at home…It's difficult to concentrate on daily routines.' I have no doubt that people in Chechnya, who have suffered bombing attacks from the Russians for more than two months at the time I am writing this, will have more severe sensations and images of their own post-traumatic memories. Indeed, studies of war and natural disasters have documented a 'dose–response curve', whereby the greater the exposure of people to traumatic events, the greater the percentage of the exposed population with symptoms of post-traumatic stress disorder.[31]

Traumatic memories often lack verbal narrative and context; rather they are made up of vivid sensations and images. Robert Jay Lifton, who has studied survivors of Hiroshima, civilian disasters and war veterans, describes the traumatic memory using phrases such as *indelible images* or *death imprints*.[32] The intense focus on image without context gives traumatic memory an amplified reality. Often one particular set of images crystallizes the experience, in what Lifton calls the 'ultimate horror'. Consider, for instance, how the Vietnam War veteran Tim O'Brien describes his traumatic memory:

> I remember the white bone of an arm. I remember the pieces of skin and something wet and yellow that must have been the intestine. The gore was horrible, and stays with me. But what wakes me up twenty years later is Dave Jensen singing 'Lemon Tree' as we threw down the parts.[33]

Unfortunately, I can readily think of a few of my own Georgian friends and colleagues who have undergone long psychiatric and psychological treatment because of the indelible images and death imprints they experienced after the tragic event that occurred in Tbilisi on 9 April 1989. This date marked the first big demonstration demanding the secession of Georgia from the Soviet Union. What began as a peaceful gathering of more than ten thousand people in front of Government House in the centre of the city ended with twenty-one dead and over five hundred injured; seventeen women were brutally slashed by a small, sharp *pehotni lopati* (a shovel), standard-issue equipment of the Russian 'Spetz group' who had arrived in Tbilisi from Russia the day before the demonstration.

The inescapable power of emotionally traumatic memories is strongly exemplified by the recollections of Holocaust survivors. In the touching book *Holocaust Testimonies: The Ruins of Memory*, Lawrence Langer writes: 'You sort of don't feel at home in this world any more, because of this experience – you can live with it, it's like constant pain: you never forget it, you never get rid of it, but you learn to live with it.' Another survivor commented: 'Part of my present life is my remembrance, my memory of what happened then, and it casts a shadow over my life today.'[34] Similar pain is apparent in the words of Ms Hoxha, a former music producer, a survivor of a massacre in Kosovo: 'I'm trying to prepare for the future, but the reality is that I'm living in the past.'[35]

With their predominance of imagery sensation, traumatic memories resemble the memories of young children. In fact, studies of children provide some of the clearest examples of traumatic memories. In one study, the child psychiatrist Lenore Terr of the University of California, San Francisco, examined children with documented histories of early trauma.[36] Although none of the children could give a verbal account of traumatic events that had occurred before they were two years old, eighteen of them showed evidence of traumatic experience in their behaviour and play. For example, one five-year-old girl did not remember the fact that she had been sexually molested by her babysitter when she was two years old. She did not remember the name of the babysitter or even the fact that she had had one. And yet Terr observed that the child in her play enacted scenes that precisely replicated the pornographic pictures found to have been made by the babysitter. This highly visual and *inactive* form of memory seems also to be mobilized in adults in situations of overwhelming terror.

Although memories of emotionally traumatic events are

generally enduring and often extraordinarily precise, they are also subject to distortion and decay. Let's consider another study by Lenore Terr, this time of the uniquely traumatic experience of Chowchilla (California) schoolchildren, who were kidnapped and abandoned in a cave for sixteen hours. This event was so traumatic that when the children were asked four years after the kidnapping what they wanted to be when they grew up, most of them replied that they never fantasized or made plans for the future because they expected to die young. The element of surprise, the threat of death and the extreme malice of the kidnappers all contributed to the severe impact of the event, even though the children were physically unharmed. Terr found that the children had the classic symptoms of traumatic memory – vivid images and recollections – both in the immediate aftermath of the event and on follow-up four years later. However, when she compared the two records – the early and late recollections of twenty-three children – she detected considerable inaccuracy and distortions in the recollections of half of the children four years after the terrifying episode (for example, one child claimed to remember two female kidnappers in addition to the male kidnappers who were actually there). Such observations demonstrate that even 'burnt-in' emotional memories are not exempt from change over time. Similar examples of traumatic memory distortion and decay in both children and adults are described in Dan Schacter's splendid book *Searching for Memory*.[37]

Nevertheless, as a rule, the central core of the experience is almost always well remembered; if distortion does occur, it is likely to involve details. It seems to me as a general principle that every time we remember something we have previously experienced, we are merely having a new present experience. We perceive and remember not as a camera reproduces on film the scenes before its lens; the scope and accuracy of our perceptions and experiences, as well as of their remembering and recall, are determined by our individual fears, joys and interests. This prior experience is not just a copy of the earlier one. Rather, we reconstruct the past experience and relive it in our present state. No wonder we cannot remember what *exactly* happened back then and there. 'Memories are not simply activated pictures in the mind but complex constructions built from multiple contributors,' proposes Schacter. This principle applies to emotionally traumatic memories as much as to any other memory recall.

| # The Flip Side of the Coin

The memory may well become confused by what is put into it, but it cannot really become surfeited. Its capacity is not reduced by receiving, any more than arranging sand into different shapes reduces its capacity to receive other shapes. In this sense the memory is bottomless.
Artur Schopenhauer

Throughout this book I have described several amnesiacs – people who for one or another reason have lost their ability to remember. The more I continued with my writing or reading about the topic, the more I realized how invaluable remembering is for maintaining a normal and fruitful life. However, imagine for a moment what it would be like if we lost the ability to forget. That is to say, if we remembered every word of every conversation, every sight, every sound, every smell, every move and every step, the colour of the eyes on every face, the shape of every cloud or every tree we encounter in our life.

A bottomless memory turns out to be a dubious blessing, as described by the distinguished Russian neuropsychologist Alexander Luria. In 1968 Luria published *The Mind of a Mnemonist*, a book about a man who suffered from the problem of being unable to forget. Luria called his patient simply S. (Shereshevsky). He followed the case of S. for some thirty years before he finally wrote:

As an experimenter, I soon found myself in a state verging on utter confusion... there was no limit either to the capacity of

S.'s memory or to the durability of the traces he retained…I
simply had to admit that I had been unable to perform what
one would think was the simplest task a psychologist can do,
measure the capacity of an individual's memory.[1]

Indeed, S. was a man with an exceptional memory capacity
who could recall verbatim a series of words, letters, numbers
or complex nonsense formulae even fifteen or sixteen years
after he had seen or read them only once. An increase in the
amount of memorized material did not cause any difficulty
for S. During the test sessions S.'s behaviour was always the
same:

> He would sit with his eyes closed, pause, then comment: 'Yes,
> yes…this was a series you gave me once when we were in
> your apartment…you were sitting at the table…you were
> wearing a grey suit…then, I can see you saying…'[2]

And then, flawlessly, S. would reproduce countless pieces of
information that had been given to him many years before.

How did he do this? What is the explanation for such
memory? Did he use the *method of loci*, the ancient
mnemonic technique described in Chapter 1? Apparently, on
some occasions he did, even though Luria never suggested
that S. was familiar with *Ad Herennium* or Cicero's writings.
To memorize a long list of words or passages, Shereshevsky,
as he explained himself, would take a 'mental walk' down
Gorky Street in Moscow, mentally placing images at houses,
gates, store windows and monuments. His images were
exceptionally 'vivid and stable', Luria writes. To recall them,
all he had to do was to initiate his 'mental walk' along the
street and 'collect' the images.

But Shereshevsky's exceptional gift held him in thrall. His

'mental walks' were not voluntary occurrences by any means – he had had them uncontrollably since early childhood and they were tremendously distracting. Words that he read or heard would often cause such graphic images and chains of recollections to develop that he was unable to finish reading a sentence or concentrate on conversations. He dealt best with concrete images and had trouble manipulating abstract concepts and thoughts. For S., as for Funes, the hero of Jorge Luis Borges's story *Funes, el Memorioso*, who remembered every single detail in his life, a dog seen in profile and the same dog seen from the front were two different dogs forming two different memories. Overwhelmed by the swarming mass of detail, S. was as handicapped as the fictional Funes. Both his personal and professional life suffered because of his never-ending flow of memories. Unable to hold down ordinary jobs, Shereshevsky – the best mnemonist ever documented – ended his days as a cheap entertainer, a 'memory man'.

Daniel Is Deep Purple

Music, when soft voices die
Vibrates in the memory –
Odours, when sweet violets sicken
Live within the sense they quicken.
Percy Bysshe Shelley

Shereshevsky's mind, however, was plagued by more than mental strolls. As Luria reported, he also possessed a profound *synaesthesia*. In synaesthesia (from the Greek *syn*, 'together', and *aisthesis*, 'perception'), stimulation of one sense gives rise to entirely unexpected responses in others. As a result, people with synaesthesia may hear numbers in colours, letters in tastes or words in smells. To one synaesthetic, the taste of chocolate is like 'pins jabbing into flesh'; to another, a particular spelling affects flavours – 'Lori' might remind a synaesthetic of the taste of a pencil, whereas 'Laurie' tastes like lemon. The most common form of the condition is when people associate letters, numbers and words with colours. The word 'Daniel', explained a synaesthetic artist from Wales, is 'deep purple, blue and red, and shiny', whereas 'Moscow' sounds more like grey with spots of green and blue.[3] In general, for synaesthetics, this is a natural part of life and they may even enjoy this exceptional quality. Vladimir Nabokov, in *Speak, Memory*, a chronological collection of reminiscences from his early childhood, describes his own 'coloured hearing' in which each sound is associated with a characteristic tint.[4] To the great Russian writer, 'o' was plain white and 'p' like an unripe, green apple. Two other Russian celebrities, the composers Scriabin and Rimski-Korsakov, heard music in colours.

For S., voices and music provoked particularly vivid sensory images and associations. A tone pitched at 30 cycles per second was like 'tarnished silver', a tone at 500 cycles per second looked like 'a stroke of lightning splitting the heavens in two', and a tone pitched at 2000 cycles per second had a 'rough and unpleasant' colour and 'an ugly taste of a briny pickle'. It remains a mystery whether for the Russian celebrities the peculiarity of synaesthesia helped in their unique creations, but for S. it was clearly an additional burden on his inability to concentrate, think and forget:

> I can't escape from seeing colors when I hear sounds. What first strikes me is the color of someone's voice. Then it fades off ... for it does interfere. If say, a person says something, I see the word; but should another person's voice break in, blurs appear. They creep into the syllables of the words and I can't

make out what is being said…It's particularly hard if there are some details in a passage I have to happen to read elsewhere. I find then that I start in one place and end up in another – everything gets muddled…My attention is distracted, and I can't get the important ideas in a passage. Even when I read about circumstances that are entirely new to me, if there happens to be a description, say, of a staircase, it turns out to be one in a house I once lived in. I start to follow it and lose the gist of what I am reading…I just can't read, can't study, for it takes up such an enormous amount of my time.[5]

It is unclear why different people are affected differently by synaesthesia. My own view is that it is the degree of the sensorial mix-up that determines who will benefit from it and who will suffer. Whilst the highest degree of synaesthesia was setting off endless chains of memories in Shereshevsky's mind, perhaps small doses of it have added poetic, artistic and musical flavours to the creations of the Russian and Welsh musicians and artists. It seems to be common for synaesthetics to have extraordinary memories; however, they generally experience difficulties with mathematics and they get lost frequently.

How and where in the brain does this sensory mix-up happen? So far, two models have been proposed. According to one model, advocated by Simon Baron-Cohen and colleagues at the London Institute of Psychiatry, the neural pathways in the synaesthetic brain are simply cross-wired. In the usual brain, the various senses are handled by neural 'modules' in specific areas of the cortex. The modules are wired together by neural pathways and the labour is divided so that information about hearing, for instance, is processed in one module, while that about smell is processed in another. In synaesthetics, unusual pathways develop linking auditory centres to taste or visual modules. So an auditory stimulus might trigger the simultaneous image of a 'rough and unpleasant' colour and the taste of a 'briny pickle'.

The American neurologist Richard Cytowic, however, does not share this view. There are no structural constructions in the brain that serve as modules, he claims, so why invent new pathways to explain synaesthesia? Cytowic proposes that all neural pathways lead to the 'emotional' brain (limbic system) after having been processed separately in the cortex. In synaesthesia, senses are mixed in the limbic system before the cortex has quite finished its work.

So far there is no strong experimental evidence for either of these proposed explanations, although probably all agree that the condition of synaesthesia is genuine and diagnosable.

Eidetikers

Thinking in terms of images was great burden for S. For a talented artist and teacher from Harvard, known to psychologists simply as 'Elizabeth', however, phenomenal ability to recall and visualize images of pictures, scenes or specific pages of poetry she had read, is no trouble. Elizabeth has the rare ability to form *eidetic* memories (from the Greek *eidos*, image).[6] The hallmark of eidetic memory is that people who have it can mentally project an exact image of a picture or scene after the original image itself is gone. They can then 'scan' the image and describe in precise detail different parts of it just as if the image were still physically present.

The most common test to identify an eidetiker involves showing a person an unfamiliar picture or printed page for thirty seconds and asking the person to recall its image. An eidetic memory differs from other forms of visual memory in that the person confidently reports that the image seems to be actually present when it is not. The phenomenon of eidetic imagery is more common in children than in adults. On the basis of the picture description method, the incidence of eidetic memory in children of elementary school age ranges from two per cent to fifteen per cent. In one particular study, the psychologist Ralph Haber at the University of Rochester in the 1960s screened some five hundred children from elementary school for eidetic image ability.[7] Children were shown a picture from *Alice's Adventures in Wonderland* and allowed to study it for a few seconds. After the picture was removed the children were asked to recall as many details of lasting image as they could. According to Haber, four per cent of children saw vivid and detailed images from which they could precisely count the stripes on a cat's tail, or the number of leaves on flowers and branches on trees.

The most remarkable eidetic imagery involves the eidetiker's capacity to form an accurate image of complex patterns of random-dot stereograms that are computer-generated. In studies performed by Charles F. Stromeyer in 1970, Elizabeth viewed a 10,000-dot pattern stereogram with her right eye through a stereoscope and then after a ten-second break she looked with her left eye at a different 10,000-dot stereogram. Ordinary people when viewing a similar pair of random-dot stereograms presented one to each eye simultaneously can superimpose the patterns and see a three-dimensional figure; but by itself each stereogram is meaningless – most of us will see nothing but thousands of murky dots. Elizabeth, however, could mentally superimpose her images of two patterns and see a letter T 'coming toward her' or a square 'floating above the surface'. An even greater feat was forming an eidetic image of a million-dot random pattern that she could retain in long-term memory for up to four hours.

It is certainly true that many people can form good visual images from memory, but no one has come close to doing what Elizabeth can do. Psychologists do not know how she developed her extraordinary ability to store such huge amounts of visual information. Similarly, so far there is no explanation for S.'s bottomless memory. So why study people with unique memory capacity? From a psychologist's point of view, the first thing to do about mnemonists is to acknowledge their existence. Whatever the explanation of their accomplishments, those accomplishments are real. Such studies will allow us to establish how many kinds of phenomenal memory abilities exist. How do such abilities develop with time? Do they wane with age? What are their frequencies in the general population or in the same family? With the answers to these questions, we would be in a better position to evaluate the ubiquitous assumption that there is a single, universally shared mechanism of memory.[8]

Chapter 6 | **The Biology of Memory**

> That which enters the mind through reason can be corrected. That which is admitted through faith, hardly ever. *Santiago Ramon y Cajal*

Anton Chekhov gave the following advice to writers: 'one must ruthlessly suppress everything that is not concerned with the subject. If, in the first chapter, you say there is a gun hanging on the wall, you should make quite sure that it is going to be used further on in the story.' Writing about the biology of memory inevitably involves the use of scientific jargon – some tongue-twisting, often Latin words, which may be overwhelming for the general reader. So I will follow Chekhov's advice to ruthlessly suppress everything, and will introduce only those terms and concepts that are necessary for basic understanding of the biology of memory and further reading of this book.

The human brain weighs only 1.5–2 kilograms but contains about 100 billion neurons. This is as many as the number of stars in the Milky Way, and roughly 1500 times more than the population of the entire UK. Santiago Ramon y Cajal, a Spanish physician and the founder of modern brain science, described neurons as 'the mysterious butterflies of the soul, the beating of whose wings may some day – who knows? – clarify the secret of mental life.'[1] Ramon y Cajal began his studies on adult and embryonic nerve cells by the end of the nineteenth century, when he came across the method developed by Camillo Golgi, the Italian anatomist, of staining neurons with silver salts. The secret of this method's success is that silver permeates some cells and turns them black but leaves the other cells untouched. Using Golgi's silver, Ramon y Cajal mapped out many of the connections of the nervous system and found that the brain was made up of discrete cells, neurons, rather than a continuous net as was thought before. For this discovery, he shared the Nobel prize in medicine in 1906 with Golgi.

Neurons are shaped like rods, spirals, shoeboxes, spheres, beans, spiders or octopuses, and they come in many different sizes. Some neurons can also specialize in a particular job. These cells, however, depend for their existence and proper function on a highly organized community life with other cells, collectively called the *neural network*. The variations in learning and memory capacities between different animals depend less on the size or shape of the neurons in their brains than on the number of neurons and the way they are interconnected. As a rule, the greater the number of neurons and the more complex their patterns of interconnection, the greater an animal's capability for flexible learning of various tasks. Every thought we have, every feeling we experience and every memory we recall occurs because of the combined action of neurons communicating with each other.

Although neurons come in various sizes and configurations, they are built according to a fundamental design that provides them with certain common features apparently necessary to live and function (Figure 6a). Every neuron has an outer wall, the membrane, which makes it a 'room' (the Latin meaning of 'cell'). At the heart of the cell body is the nucleus. The nucleus is an executive control point for the cell – a computer, construction boss and board of directors all rolled into one. Almost all the cell does is supervised by the nucleus. The nucleus houses our chromosomes, twisted curls

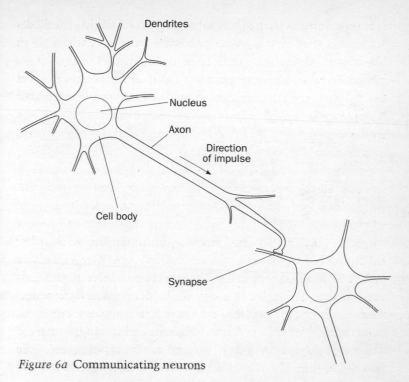

Figure 6a Communicating neurons

of deoxyribonucleic acid (DNA) – the world-renowned double helix that encodes the genetic blueprint of life and all cell function. Surrounding the nucleus is the cytoplasm, a semifluid material that contains a complex of molecular machinery for producing and packaging an army of versatile compounds called proteins. Proteins are built by joining together long chains of individual building blocks called amino acids. Although there are only twenty different amino acids, there is an astronomical number of possible combinations in a complex protein. Each protein is encoded by ribonucleic acid (RNA), a giant molecule in the cell whose synthesis is in turn under the control of the cell's genetic

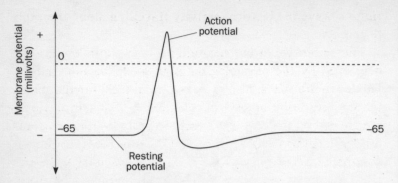

Figure 6b Membrane potential

material – DNA. So this chain is summarized as follows: DNA → RNA → protein.

The individual neuron is an ingenious device that sends and receives messages. It uses two kinds of specialized structures to do this: *dendrites*, the trees branching from the cell body, which receive chemical signals; and a single *axon*, a filament that acts as a self-powered transmission cable. The power originates in a chemical exchange between the axon and its surroundings, which sets up an electrical difference across the membrane. Normally, when a cell is resting, this difference is about minus sixty-five millivolts – the *resting membrane potential*. It results from the biochemical and physical properties of the membrane, which ensure an unequal distribution of charged chemicals (ions) such as sodium and potassium across it. When a dendrite or the cell body is stimulated by an incoming signal from another cell bringing a 'message' about (for example) a pinprick or a loud noise, the electrical difference is perturbed, causing the voltage of the membrane potential to swing rapidly up or down. Each cell receives inputs from many others. When a neuron receives enough inputs at the same time, it will fire an *action poten-*

tial – a wave of electrical activity travelling along the axon (Figure 6b).

The action potential, according to the 'ionic hypothesis' developed by the physiologists Alan Hodgkin and Andrew Huxley in the 1940s, results from a small local fluctuation in ion concentration across the membrane.[2] The fluctuations are created by the two-way traffic of sodium and potassium ions through a specific highway – the tiny pores in the cell membrane called *ion channels*. The ion channels open and close in a precise sequence along the path of the signal, creating a change in membrane potential that travels through the cell at velocities ranging from 1 to 100 metres per second. Travelling in waves along the axon, the action potential eventually arrives at the axon's end. This branches out into tiny filaments which form the presynaptic terminals.

The presynaptic terminals make contact with a dendrite of the next neuron (or a muscle or gland). The junctions where the contacts are made are called *synapses*. A typical neuron has thousands of synapses with other neurons. Arriving at the synapse, the electrical signal has 'to jump' a slight gap called the synaptic cleft. At this point a major modification happens: electricity is changed into chemistry and the pulse's arrival at the terminal releases packets of a chemical neurotransmitter. The packets, as discovered in the 1950s by Bernard Katz, the British neurophysiologist who pioneered the modern analysis of synaptic transmission, are of fixed size, each containing about 5000 molecules. The typical neurotransmitters are glutamate, gamma-aminobutyric acid (GABA), acetylcholine, noradrenaline and dopamine. The released neurotransmitters cross the gap and bind to protein molecules (receptors) on the surface of the recipient cell – the post-synaptic cell. The complete process takes no more than a fraction of a second and some of the most splendid

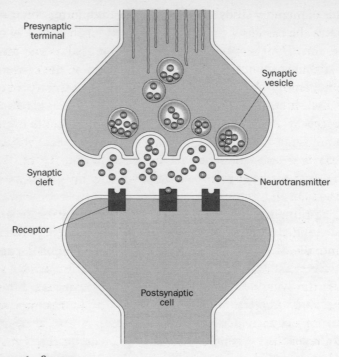

Figure 6c Synapse

activities of the brain, such as learning and memory, all perception, all movement and all emotions, emerge from this event.

The Worm Runners Digest

There are no facts, only interpretations. *Friedrich Nietzsche*

So how is the life of the neuron related to memory? And what, if anything, does DNA have to do with it? It was inevitable that once a mechanism for the genetic transmission of information was recognized as being embedded in the DNA, researchers would sooner or later extend its influence into the fields of memory study. If DNA, the master information molecule, is the carrier of the genetic memory for the shape of our face, the colour of our eyes, the curls of our palms and many other things about us, why could it not also be the carrier of brain memory? Admittedly, we do not inherit memories of our parents' lifetimes. But could not our own memories be encoded by RNA or amino acids? Or maybe there is even a unique small protein molecule for each of our recollections? These were the thoughts at the beginning of 1960s. The misguided enthusiasm was further stirred up by developments in the field of immunology.

The immune system has an ability to manufacture molecules called antibodies. Antibodies are proteins that can surround, attack and inactivate unfamiliar or foreign molecules. But their real gift is to retain a 'memory' of the intruder and boost the body's ability to recognize and inactivate it on a later raid. Genetic memory, conventional memory and immunological memory probably have much in common, and presumably a single mechanism is responsible for the working of all three, suggested I. B. Meckler in the journal *Nature*, in 1967.[3] Similar descriptions also crop up in other publications.

> Individual molecules are the fundamental decision-making elements in the brain...the function of the neuron is to allow the elements to communicate with one another.[4]

> In this paper, animal behaviour, in particular learning and memory, has been reduced to the behaviour of proteins, whether individual or assembled in superstructures...the interplay of billions of such molecular events, ensured by appropriate wiring, brings about complex forms of learning in animals and in man.[5]

So if memories are stored as molecules, then the brain should accumulate gigantic quantities of these molecules over a life-time, and eventually the conspicuous memory molecules might be extracted from the brain. Imagine that they could then be syn-thesized in a laboratory and perhaps sold in a local health-food shop. You could go in and buy whichever memory molecule you wanted – Mendelssohn's *Rondo capriccioso*; Dante's *Paradiso*; *Memories of a Saint* by Magritte; or Einstein's theory of relativ-ity. Perhaps they could even come in different colours: extra or mild strengths, kid or adult sizes. Who knows, maybe this was the hope when a series of attention-absorbing experiments in 'memory transfer' began to be performed.[6]

The star in these experiments was a humble, simple-minded flatworm, a planarian. The originator of this research was the psychologist James McConnell. In the 1960s, at the University of Michigan in Ann Arbor, his worms became so popular and exotic that they merited a mystically named journal, *The Worm Runners Digest*, all to themselves. First McConnell trained a group of worms to arch or scrunch in response to a flashing light paired with an electric shock. After several rounds of this manipulation, the worms had mastered their lesson and began arching at the sight of light alone. Then he cut up their bodies and allowed the other, inexperienced worms to cannibalize them. Sure enough, McConnell claimed, the cannibal worms absorbed memory molecules along with their educated tutors: when tested, they behaved as if they 'remembered' that flashing lights predicted an electric shock. He advertised his findings under such titles as 'Memory transfer through cannibalism in planarians' for another two decades, before quietly vanishing from the scene when other scientists failed to replicate his results.

Three years after the first cannibal worms, rats that could 'transfer' memory molecules began to appear. In 1965,

F. R. Babich together with McConnell's pupil Allan Jacobson reported in the journal *Science* that they had achieved a transfer effect. They taught a group of rats to run to a food container in response to a clicking sound, then guillotined them and extracted RNA from their brains. They injected this now 'educated' RNA into the intestines of their uneducated buddies who began to react to a click by approaching the food container even though the container was empty. Based on these results, Jacobson and colleagues assumed that RNA was the memory carrier.

At the same time, Georges Ungar and Oceguera-Navarro at the University of Texas in Houston used an extract from the brains of rats accustomed to the sound of a hammer dropping on a metal plate. This extract, claimed the researchers, facilitated the adaptation of mice to the same stimulus when injected into their guts. But the most dramatic series of planarian-style experiments were still to come.

In the 1970s, Georges Ungar abandoned his hammer-dropping experiments and instead trained rats in a passive avoidance or step-through task. Rats or mice are naturally nocturnal creatures, preferring dark surroundings to a light environment. Ungar trained his rats to inhibit their inclinations and avoid the dark by delivering an electric shock when they entered a dark portion of a training box; this punishment resulted in the refusal of the 'anti-dark' animals to enter the dark compartment. He then injected brain extracts from the trained rats into untrained animals who promptly showed fear of the dark when given a straightforward light/dark choice. From the brains of a few thousand rats that had been trained to fear the dark, Ungar and his group eventually purified the component that, they claimed, carried the information about 'fear of the dark'. Ungar's 'memory' molecule was a small protein (peptide) and he named it 'scotophobin' –

from the Greek *scotos* (darkness) and *phobos* (fear). Ungar and his colleagues went on to isolate more 'memory' molecules; anelatin was isolated from the brains of rats taught to respond to the sound of an electric bell, and chromodiopsin was isolated from the brains of thousands of goldfish trained to distinguish between blue and green colours.

Memory transfer experiments provoked a frantic controversy in the research field, with many scientists failing to repeat them successfully. A letter signed by twenty-three researchers from seven laboratories across the USA appeared in *Science*, reporting that in eighteen experiments no clear evidence had been obtained of a transfer of any of these kinds of training from trained donors to recipients. Memory molecules fell out of fashion in the early 1970s, and today most scientists have abandoned the idea that each memory is encoded by a single protein. As Steven Rose, a leading neuroscientist at the Open University in the UK, in his acclaimed book *The Making of Memory*, put it: 'If there were such memory peptides and each was present in the brain in the concentration of scotophobin, then to code for the memories of the human lifetime would demand that the brain contained a mass of peptides weighing something of the order of 100 kilograms – or rather more than the weight of an average human.'[7]

Synapse at Work

What is research, but a blind date with knowledge? *Will Henry*

The neural junctions were labelled *synapses* by the neurophysiologist Charles Sherrington in 1897.[8] Twenty-five years previously, however, a philosopher, Alexander Bain, had suggested that memory formation involves communication at such a junction:

For every act of memory, every exercise of bodily aptitude, every habit, recollection, trade of ideas, there is a specific grouping or coordination of sensations and movements, by virtue of specific growths in the cell junctions.[9]

Similarly, the neurologist Eugenio Tanzi, in 1893, proposed that the passage of a nervous impulse during learning could cause a neuron to lengthen its cytoplasmic fibres. With additional activating stimuli, the fibres could grow even closer to the recipient cells, making conduction across the synapse and cell-to-cell communication even more likely. A year later, Ramon y Cajal proposed in his Croonian lecture to the Royal Society:

Mental exercise facilitates a greater development of...the nervous collaterals in the part of the brain in use. In this way, pre-existing connections between groups of cells could be reinforced by multiplication of the terminal branches...the cerebral cortex is like a garden planted with innumerable trees – the pyramidal cells – which, thanks to intelligent cultivation, can multiply their branches and sink their roots deeper, producing fruits and flowers of ever greater variety and quality.[10]

Ramon y Cajal predicted that as we learn something, the patterns and strengths of electrical signals that constitute our brain's activity should change. As a result of this changed activity, neurons become capable of modulating communication with one another. The persistence of these alternations in neuronal communication – called *plasticity* – might be the key to the mechanism of memory storage.

Such speculations were put on a firmer basis by Donald Hebb, one of the most influential psychologists of his time, whose book *The Organization of Behaviour*, published in 1949, became a keystone of modern neuroscience. Born in Chester, a small fishing town on the coast of Nova Scotia, Hebb began his adult life intending to be a novelist. Realizing that his calling required an understanding of psychology, and intrigued by the works of Sigmund Freud, Hebb applied to the psychology department of McGill University, where he was accepted in 1928 as a part-time graduate student. What started out as a temporary interest quickly became a career.

Hebb's career in psychology was long and diverse. He was one of the first to observe the social behaviour of captive porpoises and to discover that they are just as intelligent as chimpanzees. With Wilder Penfield, an eminent neurosurgeon and founder of the Montreal Neurological Institute, he studied intellectual changes in patients after brain damage. But most of all, Hebb was involved in the nature–nurture controversy and investigated the effects of environment on intelligence in humans and other species, designing experiments to test his contention that animals raised in enriched environments would be able to profit by new experiences at maturity. In one instance, he allowed some of his laboratory rats to explore his home for weeks as pets of his children and then returned them to the laboratory. They were better at subsequently learning a variety of tests than their unlucky peers who had not been invited into Hebb's house but had instead remained in their laboratory cages. He also carried out isolation experiments, in which generously paid volunteer students were kept in sensory deprivation booths for as long as they could endure it (none of them lasted even a week). He attached electrodes to the students' skulls to record their brain waves, and supplied them with a microphone to report their experiences. The volunteers' ability to think began to deteriorate, and some of them even started to hallucinate.[11]

However, Hebb is best known for his 'Hebbian rules of association', which allow the 'translation' of associated behavioural phenomena into a neural mechanism. The basic idea is this. When a cell is activated by a learning event, for example, neurons begin to communicate with each other – they send signals to 'fire' or not to 'fire'. These synaptic events cause groups of interconnected neurons to set into motion a reverberating electrical signal, just like twinkling lights on a Christmas tree. In reality, there are many neurons involved in a series of circuits, with each neuron receiving signal inputs from several other neurons simultaneously. The short-term memory for an event is achieved for as long as the neural network continues to reverberate. But how do we get long-term memory out of this blueprint?

Hebb believed that if uninterrupted for long enough, a reverberating circuit of interacting neurons should strengthen.

> When an axon of cell A is near enough to excite a cell B and repeatedly and persistently takes part in firing it, some growth process or metabolic changes takes place in one or both cells such that A's efficiency, as one of the cells firing B, is increased.[12]

In other words, co-activation of connected cells should result in a modification of their connection, increasing the probability that the recipient cell will fire if the presynaptic cell does so. This makes eminently good sense, because it allows for associated world events to be represented by cell-to-cell interactions.

Physical changes accompanying cell-to-cell interactions could take many different forms. For example, more receptors in the post-synaptic membrane could bind with neurotransmitters; synaptic strength between neurons could increase (that is, it might become easier for one neuron to excite neighbouring neurons); new synapses could form between neurons; and so on. When the anatomical changes are achieved, the memory becomes permanent.

Enrichment and Impoverishment

The expression often used by Mr Herbert Spencer of the Survival of the Fittest, is more accurate, and is sometimes equally convenient.
Charles Darwin

Exercise and strengthen your muscles, advised Dr McCormick after my back surgery. Indeed, we know that just as hard labour thickens the skin, trained and used muscles become stronger. But does mental exercise change the structure of the brain? Does learning enlarge particular brain regions?

The possibility of testing experimentally whether training can affect the growth of the brain was first discussed in 1783 in a correspondence between the Swiss naturalist Charles Bonnet and the Piedmontese anatomist Michele Malacarne. To test the hypothesis, Malacarne ran an experiment with two litter-mate dogs and a pair of birds. In each pair, he intensively trained one animal but not the other. After a few years of treatment, both experienced and inexperienced animals were killed and Malacarne compared their brains. He claimed that trained animals had more folds in the cerebrum than their untrained litter-mates (in humans, the cerebrum comprises two-thirds of the brain and is responsible for storing most of our personal memories). About 170 years elapsed, however, before training and experience were proved to produce measurable neuroanatomical and biochemical changes in the brain.

Inspired by Hebb's ideas about the nature–nurture controversy, Mark Rosenzweig and his colleagues at the University of California at Berkeley began experiments in the late 1950s to find changes in the brain induced by training or experience.[13] Instead of training rats in a variety of problem-solving tasks, Rosenzweig and his co-workers housed and raised the animals in two different environments that provided different opportunities for informal learning. In the basic experimental design one group of animals were raised in an environment that featured other rats, as well as various mind-broadening items such as ladders, rotating wheels and toys which were changed daily. A comparable set of rats were raised in isolation, living in individual cages with a little illumination and nothing for entertainment other than plenty of food and water. The first environment was called 'enriched', although such a term is surely an exaggeration when one considers the way real rats live in California (thousands nest in the palm trees that grace the streets of Los Angeles, and, at times, a rat or two will fall from the bushy-headed palm into a passing convertible, altering the consciousness of the driver). The second environment was called 'impoverished'.

Rosenzweig's group found that after several weeks of rearing the rats in these contrasting environments, the cerebral cortex of the 'enriched' rats weighed four per cent more than the cortex of the 'impoverished' (though fatter) rats. Differential experience also caused changes in cortical chemistry; enriched experience led to increased amounts of cortical enzymes, especially those responsible for regulation of neurotransmitters that carry signals across the synapses between neighbouring nerve cells.

The initial reports by Rosenzweig's team were greeted with scepticism. Hebb even cautioned Rosenzweig that the more important the claims, the more careful should be the tests. Over the next several years, however, related research flourished and branched out in several directions, leading to important discoveries. The differences in brain weight were not uniformly distributed throughout the cerebral cortex: crucially, the largest increase in brain weight was in the portions of the brain that serve visual perception, presumably those that had been particularly stimulated in the enriched environment. This was clear evidence that learning or experience causes changes in specific brain regions, and not random growth of brain.

Soon after publication of the Rosenzweig team's findings came another kind of evidence of cortical plasticity. Two Nobel prizewinners, David Hubel and Torsten Wiesel, reported that in a kitten, depriving one eye of light, starting at the age at which the eyes first open, reduced the number of cortical cells that respond to subsequent stimulation of that eye.[14] Further findings revealed that plasticity of the visual cortex could be restored by treating animals with neurotransmitters such as acetylcholine or noradrenaline.

The learning of birdsong also provided some intriguing findings. As a part of his fascinating study of the songs of male canaries, Fernando Nottebohm at the Rockefeller University at New York correlated the size of two specific regions in the bird's brain with singing. He found that during the most active vocal periods, these two regions may double in size compared with that during the least active period, the summer moult. Later in the year, new nerve fibres and fresh synapses develop, the brain grows larger and a grand song repertoire originates once again.[15]

Even birds who are not gifted with musical talents, such as day-old chicks, have the capacity for similar plastic changes in the nervous system.[16] A group of British scientists at the Open University headed by Steven Rose trained chicks to peck or not to peck a shiny chrome bead coated with either plain water or a bitter-tasting liquid called methylanthranilate (when I worked with Steven we used to label them as 'W' and 'M' chicks). As a rule, a single peck is enough for methylanthranilate-trained chicks to refuse to have anything to do with chrome beads. Although just one day old, these funny, fluffy creatures form a good and long-lasting memory of a distasteful bead: any time they see the shiny bead after training, they will vigorously avoid it by shaking their head, closing their eyes, running or cheeping for help. (Such robust response finally provoked Steven to taste the 'M' bead himself. I believe the memory of this experience is firmly laid down in Steven's synapses too.) Chicks with memories of methylanthranilate on their minds had about sixty per cent more dendritic branches in a particular brain region than the 'W' chicks. Long-term memory of this bitter compound seems to leave its signature across synapses.

Other specific brain changes have been reported. Fred Gage and colleagues at the Salk Institute for Biological Studies in La Jolla, California, have demonstrated how day-to-day activities change the weight of the brain.[17] These researchers exposed mice to a playground environment with multi-door tunnels, and assortment of plastic tubes, papers and a variety of nesting materials. The 'enriched mice' were found to have about 40,000 more neurons in the hippocampus. The hippocampus, which as we have seen has an important role in memory, seems to function even better if bigger: the enriched mice were better at solving problems in memory-challenging maze tasks than their companions raised in spartan conditions. Similarly, species of the crow family that store food in many different places for future use develop a larger hippocampus than related species that do not store food. Even more intriguingly, the difference in the hippocampal size is not found in young birds still in the nest; it appears only after food storing has started and the memory of the location has formed. This is consistent with the hippocampus's crucial role in spatial memory, as described in Chapter 3.

But bigger is not always better. *Aplysia*, an extensively studied mollusc, seems to store its simple memories by either decreasing or increasing the numbers of synapses. The synaptic changes induced by learning and memory also occur in rodents, cats and monkeys.[18] As noted by William Greenough of the University of Illinois, 'experience-dependent synaptic plasticity is more widely reported, in terms of species, than any other putative memory mechanisms.'[19]

However, most memory researchers are concerned with how synaptic changes can store information and how neural circuits can compute memories. The two most popular and successful model approaches during the past thirty years have been the study of the cellular correlates of learning and memory in the sea slug *Aplysia*, and the study of a physiological phenomenon called long-term potentiation. Let's consider them in turn.

Simple Memories of Simple Organisms: *Aplysia* the Sea Slug

I am as my Creator made me, and since He is satisfied, so am I.
Minnie Smith

About once a week a colourful box labelled 'Live tropical fish' arrives at the Center for Neurobiology and Behavior at Columbia University, New York, from Miami. The shipment is delivered to an animal house on the ninth floor – a room with a big rectangular aquarium along the wall. There, the tropical beauties are freed to swim in salty water. But the new arrivals do not have long to live. A day or two later, a scientist will scoop up one of them and transport it in a plastic bag filled with water to a laboratory, where its life ends in a

small Petri dish. These creatures are the stars of cell learning
and memory research – *Aplysia californica*.

Aplysia is not a beauty at all. It is a splotchy, purple-
brownish sea slug about the size of a cantaloupe and the
shape of a turtle without the shell. If not caught for laboratory use, *Aplysia* lives on the sea floor near the beach and
grazes on sea lettuce. Charles Darwin, the father of the greatest intellectual revolution of our time, when on his famous
voyage on the *Beagle*, noticed *Aplysia* in the waters off the
island of St Jago: they are, Darwin wrote, 'a dirty yellowish
colour, veined with purple', and when disturbed they spew
out a sticky, purplish ink. They smell disgusting and probably taste disgusting too, because almost nothing will eat
them.

What made *Aplysia* a celebrated slug? How has this
simple-minded mollusc managed to contribute to our
insights into the biology of learning? If I started to describe
all the achievements in our understanding of the cellular
mechanisms of learning and memory gained from studies of
this slug, I would end up by writing a book called *Memoir of
Aplysia*, or something similar. And if I chose to do so, this
would be just a poor reflection of what the Columbia
University professor and Nobel prizewinner of 2000, Eric
Kandel, has been brilliantly doing himself over the past four
decades. Many scientists and science writers have devoted
sizeable chunks of their books and papers to describing
Kandel's work on the neuronal and molecular processes
underlying *Aplysia*'s scholastic achievements: some give
sober critical accounts of the topic, others sing the praise of
Aplysia and its master. I therefore shall limit myself by
outlining only some of the basic findings.

The chief advantage of *Aplysia*, from the neurobiological
point of view, is its simple nervous system, which consists of

just 20,000 nerve cells, compared with the 100 billion neurons of a human brain. Furthermore, many of the neurons are conveniently large and distinctive (some of them are nearly a millimetre in diameter and can even be seen by the naked eye). This means that the same cells can be identified from animal to animal, in both trained and non-trained slugs, and compared to see what sort of neuronal or molecular changes, if any, are caused by training. The neurons are collected into distinct groups called ganglia, and each ganglion usually consists of a few hundred neurons. This numerical simplification has allowed scientists to study the function of individual cells and to relate their function to behaviour.[20] If you wish to understand the cellular details of learning, Kandel and colleagues reasoned, why not study the simplest biological system that can answer your questions? With this in mind, Kandel's team proceeded to draw a painstaking cell-by-cell wiring diagram of *Aplysia*'s nervous system.[21]

As humans, we by no means want to be compared to simple-minded *Aplysia*, and yet we share many common behavioural patterns with this animal, including some elementary perceptual and motor coordination, or classical conditioning. In addition, no fundamental differences in structure, chemistry or function are apparent between the neurons and synapses of a human and those of a snail. These similarities suggest that the neuronal mechanisms for some learning processes may have features in common from one species to another.

If anything touches *Aplysia*'s siphon – the organ that sucks oxygen-loaded water over the slug's breathing apparatus, the gill – it contracts and the gill withdraws hastily into a little mantle (Figure 7a). This is a simple defensive withdrawal reflex that protects the delicate respiratory organ from damage. This reflex is like the withdrawal response that we

David, Enrico
David, Jacques-Louis
Davies, Peter
Davis, Peter
Dawson, Verne
De Maria, Walter
De Rivera, José
De Stijl
Deacon, Richard
Dean, Tacita
Debord, Guy
Degas, Edgar
Delacroix, Eugene
Delaunay, Robert
Delaunay, Sonia
Deller, Jeremy
Demand, Thomas
Denes, Agnes
diCorcia, Phillipe-Lorca
Di Cosimo, Piero
Dieroff, Xenia
Dijkstra, Rineke
Dine, Jim
Dion, Mark
Dix, Otto
Docherty, Willie
Dogon art
Doig, Peter
Donachie, Kay
Donagh, Rita
Donatello
Donegan, Cheryl
Drummond, Fiona
Dubossarsky and Vinogradov
Dubuffet, Jean
Duchamp, Marcel
Dufy, Raoul
Dumas, Marlene

Dunham, Carroll
Durham, Jimmy

E

Edmier, Keith
Eggleston, William
Egyptian art
Eichmann, Volker
Eisenman, Nicole
El Greco
Elgin marbles
Eliasson, Olafur
Elizabethan miniatures
Emin, Tracey
Enlightenment
Ensor, James
Entartete Kunst
Epstein, Jacob
Escher, MC
Espaliu, Pepe
Etruscan art
Evans, Walker
Expressionism

F

Fabre, Jan
Fahlström, Öyvind
Faier, Jonathan
Fairhurst, Angus
Fairnington, Mark
Faithfull, Simon
Fanni Tutti, Cosey
Farquhar, Keith
Fauvism
Fecteau, Vincent
Feinstein, Rachel
Feminism
Fend, Peter

all experience when we jerk our hand away after touching a hot object. When Kandel and his colleagues wanted to 'teach' *Aplysia*, they took advantage of this inborn reflex. Typically, in this experiment, the researcher touches the siphon with a little brush, causing both siphon and gill to withdraw quickly. However, after about ten touches, the creature learns to ignore the now familiar stimulus, and the animal shows little or no withdrawal of the gill. The process by which an animal becomes accustomed to the stimulus to the point of ignoring it is called habituation. We all have this capacity.

An extreme example of human habituation, known as 'Bowery-el phenomenon', is described by Karl Pribram in *Languages of The Brain*:

> For many years, there was an elevated railway line (the 'el') on Third Avenue in New York that made a fearful racket; when it was torn down, people who had been living in apartments along the line awakened periodically out of a sound sleep to call the police about some strange occurrence they could not properly define. The calls were made at the times the trains had formerly rumbled past. The strange occurrences were, of course, the deafening silence that had replaced the expected noise.[22]

Habituated to the sounds of train wheels, the Bowery 'el' neighbours became 'sensitized' to silence. Sensitization is the flip side of habituation: an enhanced response to a stimulus, even to a harmless one. *Aplysia* is gifted with this talent as well. If it receives a brief electric shock to its tail, then its reaction to siphon stimulation is substantially strengthened. A few rounds of this procedure and the horrified slug soon pulls its gill under the full protection of the mantle shelf.

Both habituation and sensitization are examples of nonassociative learning and are universal properties of all organisms with a nervous system. The duration of the memory for habituation or sensitization depends on the intensity of the training. For example, if only one stimulus is applied to the slug, the memory for the stimulus is short-lived – lasting about ten to fifteen minutes. However, if the procedures causing habituation or sensitization are repeated for a few days, the memory will last for two to three weeks – an example of long-term memory in the slug. What Ebbinghaus found for the learning of syllables – practice makes memory perfect – seems to work in *Aplysia* as well.

So what goes on in *Aplysia*'s nerve cells when these memories form? To address the question, Kandel and his team began to work out the wiring diagram of the gill-withdrawal reflex. The neural circuit of this behaviour appeared to be humble. The researchers identified six motor cells innervating the gill and seven motor cells innervating the siphon. These motor cells receive commands about what to do and when to do it directly from about forty sensory neurons that innervate the siphon skin. To add a bit of complexity, the sensory neurons also form connections with excitatory and inhibitory interneurons that, in turn, project to the motor cells. So once you touch the slug's siphon, the sensory neurons activate the gill and siphon motor neurons; the defensive behaviour will be initiated (Figure 7b).

If the neural circuit of the defensive reflex is so pre-wired, so predetermined and so perfectly well set, then how can learning change it? How can memory occur and be stored in such a circuit? What sort of plastic modifications will contribute to memory storage? Kandel and colleagues seem to have found an answer: even though the neural circuit for the gill-withdrawal reflex is set once and for all early in development, the strength of the connection between the cells is not.

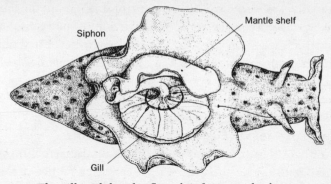

Figure 7a The gill-withdrawl reflex of *Aplysia* results from stimulation of the siphon

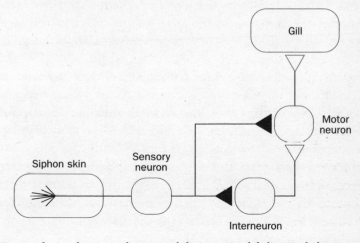

Figure 7b A schematic diagram of the circuit of defensive behaviour

The strength of a connection can be studied by recording the synaptic activity. For this purpose the slug was dissected and the sensory and motor cells were isolated. The simplified '*Aplysia*' was placed on a dish under a microscope, and microelectrodes inserted into its large neurons. These microelectrodes are tiny fluid-filled glass probes, or metal wires, with tips less than one thousandth of a centimetre in diameter, which when inserted into a neuron can either pick up or deliver signals to individual cells and reveal some of the electrical processes that take place there. 'Learning in a dish' is in this way initiated.[23] The researchers simulated the habituation training procedure by electrically stimulating the sensory neurons with the same time intervals used for the intact animal. They observed a dramatic weakening in the strength of the synaptic connection as a result of short-term habituation. This weakening – Kandel's team claimed – results from a decrease in the number of packets of neurotransmitter released by each action potential. The entire process appeared to depend on calcium levels – the ion necessary for the generation of an action potential in the presynaptic terminal.

If memory for short-term habituation only caused short-term, transient changes in synaptic strength, what happens when slugs go through a long-term habituation procedure? Would long-term habituation inactivate a previously functioning synapse? It seems so. Long-term habituation causes prolonged and profound change in synapses, leading to disruption of most of the previously effective connections. Importantly, sensitization leads to an increase in the number of synaptic connections within the neural circuit for the gill-withdrawal reflex.

These studies clearly illustrate that the same set of synaptic connections can be modulated in opposite directions by different forms of learning – habituation and sensitization. They provide important experimental evidence supporting Ramon y Cajal's early idea that the synaptic connections are not fixed but can be modified by training. These modifications in synaptic strength persist, and most probably serve the function of memory storage. But what is even more fascinating is that this simple animal, or to be precise its neuronal preparation, enables us to uncover various steps of the molecular processes crucial for learning and memory in higher vertebrates. It therefore provides a good model to study cellular and molecular aspects of some types of learning and memory. Some of them I will consider in the last chapter.

Long-term Potentiation

Research is the process of going up alleys to see if they are blind.
Marston Bates

The most frequently used word by President Bill Clinton during his four-hour three-minute testimony in front of the grand jury was 'remember'. The most frequently used equivalent of 'remember' among memory researchers is LTP: this is the acronym for 'long-term potentiation', a phenomenon first described in 1973 by Terje Lomo and Tim Bliss, at that time working in Per Andersen's laboratory in Oslo.[24] Intrigued by the role of the hippocampus in declarative memory (described in Chapter 3) as well as the well-defined synaptic circuitry of the hippocampus, Bliss and Lomo began to search for the neural mechanism of learning and memory within the neural circuits of this structure (Figure 8a). They anaesthetized a rabbit and implanted microelectrodes into its hippocampus. One electrode (the stimulating electrode) was placed into the perforant pathway – one of the three major synaptic pathways in the hippocampus. This pathway projects from the entorhinal cortex, the main source of information to the hippocampus, to the dentate gyrus, an area of the hippocampus filled with oval cells known as granule cells. This is where the other electrode, the recording electrode, was placed. Bliss and Lomo then repeatedly stimulated the perforant pathway with a brief train of electrical impulses and observed a sharp and surprisingly persistent increase in the efficiency of synaptic transmission. This enhanced synaptic strength can last as long as 120 days in an alert, freely moving animal. The duration and location of LTP immediately intrigued almost everyone in the field of memory research. The popularity of LTP grew further when it was found not only in intact animals, but also in preparations *in vitro* (when a brain is dissected and recordings are made from thin hippocampal slices). Might this phenomenon be a cellular representation of our memories, or at least certain forms of memory? After all, there are not many other candidates with the correct properties.

The assumption that information is stored in the brain as changes in synaptic strength originated more than a century ago. If so, then the location of storage, the engram of memory, must be found among experienced synapses, those that have undergone changes in synaptic efficiency because of their activity during learning. Thus, in the past twenty-five years, LTP in the hippocampus has become a celebrated neuronal player, the dominant model for memory. The nuances of this model have even been described in different flavours: 'vanilla LTP', 'chocolate LTP' and even 'strawberry LTP'.[25]

But let's pause and consider the properties of LTP that have captured the imagination of neuroscientists for such a long time. First, in addition to its remarkably long duration, LTP is pathway-specific: the potentiation is confined to active synapses, that is, the synapses to which the electrical stimulation is delivered. Other synapses on the same cell will not be activated. The second property is called 'cooperativity' and describes the rules for the induction of LTP: LTP is triggered when *many* fibres are activated in synchrony by a

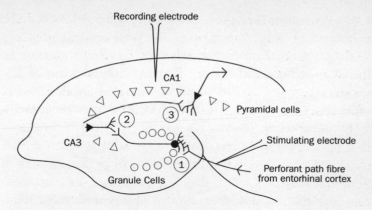

Figure 8a A schematic diagram of the *in vitro* hippocampal slice showing stimulating and recording sites

'strong' electrical stimulus or when a 'weak' stimulus is applied to an *individual* fibre, although a stimulus has to be coupled to an active state of a recipient cell. Similarly, a train of high-frequency pulses can produce LTP, while pulses delivered slowly are almost ineffective. So to induce LTP one has to work out a complex pattern of electrical stimulation. Once this is accomplished and LTP is induced, it may proceed through a few stages until it culminates with a late phase (L-LTP), which – like long-term memory – requires the synthesis of new proteins.

The third and perhaps most alluring feature of LTP as a cellular device for memory is associativity. Long-term potentiation is associative in the sense that a 'weak' stimulus incapable of triggering LTP in its own right may be supported and potentiated if it is active while a strong conditioning train arrives from a separate pathway. Associativity provides a cellular model of classical conditioning and is a key property of the Hebb synapse, as I described earlier in this chapter. The two contributing inputs need to be active simultaneously, just as the conditioning and the unconditioned stimuli have to be combined for associative learning.

How are these properties achieved and how can they be explained at the cellular level? To answer these questions scientists looked at the neurotransmitters, receptors and proteins that underlie the intimate details of cell behaviour. A great deal of understanding has now been achieved, especially in hippocampal slice preparations. In the hippocampus, the major neural pathways use the amino acid glutamate as their neurotransmitter. Glutamate is released from the tip of the axon of a presynaptic neuron into the synaptic cleft, flows across the gap and binds to receptors on the dendrites of the post-synaptic cell. But the interaction of glutamate with the recipient cell is not simple: there are at least two different types of glutamate receptor on the recipient cell, each with its own pattern of distribution among cells sensitive to glutamate, each with its own pharmacological characteristics and each producing specific types of post-synaptic responses. These are the NMDA and non-NMDA receptors. The NMDA receptor (so called for its ability to bind a glutamate analogue, N-methyl-D-aspartate) turns out to be the crucial component for plasticity. Non-NMDA receptors dominate most synaptic transmission, because the ion channel associated with the NMDA receptor is usually firmly plugged by magnesium ions. But when the cell is sufficiently excited, magnesium ions tend to drift out of the pore and the NMDA channel is open for business: if glutamate now binds to the receptor, calcium flows through the open door into the cell and LTP is initiated (Figure 8b).

If glutamate is the 'first violin' in the orchestra, then calcium is the 'conductor'. When calcium enters the cell it triggers a sequence of biochemical events that culminates in increase of synaptic power. One of the first biochemical steps

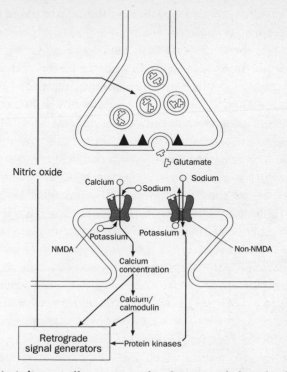

Figure 8b A diagram illustrating molecular events believed to be responsible for LTP in at least one part of the hippocampus

leading to LTP following calcium entry into the post-synaptic cell is the binding of calcium to a cytoplasmic protein called calmodulin. The shape of calmodulin is reminiscent of a flower with four petals, which attracts and binds four calcium molecules, much like a flower attracts a bee. Calmodulin then changes its shape to enable the newly formed calcium–calmodulin complex to bind other proteins, collectively known as protein kinases. Protein kinases, in turn, activate other proteins by a process called phosphorylation (an act of binding of phosphate ions to a protein).

Calcium initiates LTP by activating different types of protein kinases such as protein kinase C (PKC), alpha-calcium-calmodulin kinase II (αCaMKII) and others.

It is possible to visualize the increased calcium in neurons following electric stimulation using special imaging techniques. Different-coloured dyes are pumped through the tip of a tiny glass electrode into the cell and a sophisticated confocal microscope allows the activity of calcium (its movement and concentration) to be scanned. The time course of these events is surprisingly long: the NMDA channel stays open for about 100–200 milliseconds, and the LTP-induced rise in calcium may persist for a few minutes. This led some researchers to speculate that this time allows the system to coordinate learning events and so plays a special role in associative memory.

So far everything we have described has taken place in the recipient cell. Although we know about the initial events underlying the induction of LTP, the mechanisms responsible for its maintenance remain unclear. Researchers have claimed many and varied results: some, for instance, have measured the amount of glutamate from the hippocampus before and after the induction of LTP and interpreted an increase in release as evidence for a presynaptic role of LTP maintenance; others have monitored the sensitivity of hippocampal neurons to different pharmacological agents that either promote or block LTP, and favoured the idea that post-synaptic modifications are important in the maintenance of LTP. To give something of the flavour of the diversity of conclusions, I will cite a paper by Tim Bliss and Graham Collingridge, published in *Nature* in 1993:

> Results of the more recent studies of fluctuations in the amplitude of synaptic responses have produced conclusions ranging from purely presynaptic, to predominantly presynaptic, to

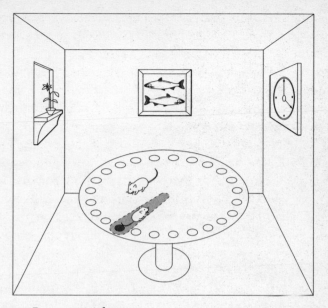

Figure 9a Barnes spatial maze

purely postsynaptic and finally, to a mixture of purely presynaptic, purely postsynaptic and both pre- and postsynaptic.

'Much ado' is likely to be happening on both sides of the synapse. If so, and the presynaptic cell is involved in the maintenance of LTP, then some messenger must be sent from the recipient cell to the presynaptic cell to deliver the instruction, 'initiate the maintenance of LTP'. A few candidates have been proposed but only one of them has attracted sustained interest.

By the beginning of the 1990s several groups of researchers had reported that nitric oxide might be such a messenger. Nitric oxide, a colourless, short-lived gas with a simple chemical formula (NO) and a reputation as an air pollutant, is the first gas to be shown to act as a signal molecule. Nitric oxide

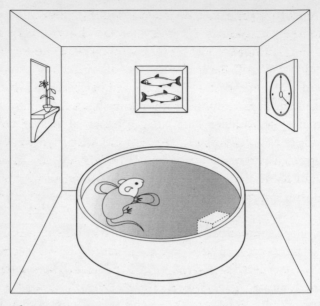

Figure 9b Morris water maze

has applications for treating conditions ranging from heart disease to shock to impotence. The discoverers of the role of nitric oxide, Robert Furchgott, Louis Ignarro and Ferid Murad, were awarded a Nobel prize in 1998 for their work on nitric oxide as a signalling molecule in the cardiovascular system, but became known to Internet fans as the three US discoverers of the Viagra principle. In the brain, nitric oxide appears to be an equally intriguing and stimulating molecule. Exposure of neurons to nitric oxide increases transmitter release from presynaptic neurons, whereas blocking the synthesis of nitric oxide in the recipient neuron wipes out LTP.

Animal Behaviour and LTP

While the debate about the key candidate for a messenger

continued to rage, researchers addressed the question of the relationship between LTP and memory by studying the behaviour of animals. The first demonstration came in a test devised by Carol Barnes, working at the University of Colorado. The Barnes maze is a circular, brightly illuminated platform surface, a couple of metres in diameter (Figure 9a). The maze has a hidden dark tunnel, which is located under only one of the many holes that surround the periphery of the platform. The maze is located in a room whose walls contain distinguishable orienting cues; so on the west wall there may be a poster, on the south a ball, on the north a clock, and so on.

A rat or a mouse placed in the centre of this illuminated open space runs at random until it locates the dark tunnel, more or less accidentally, and hides in it. A video camera mounted above the maze can track the path taken by the running animal. Young and healthy rats will run more or less directly to the tunnel after just a few trials (rats' closest relatives, mice, are considerably slower in locating the tunnel). They find it by distinct cues in the environment, such as the poster, ball or clock. Ageing, however, profoundly affects a rat's capacity to remember the spatial cues and therefore dramatically impairs its ability to find a direct escape route in the circular maze. So Barnes reasoned that if LTP-like phenomena underlie the mechanism of memory storage, then old rats, with defects in spatial memory, might show poor LTP. Sure enough, she found that the old animals who performed worst on the spatial task also had the fastest decaying potentiation.

The second impressive demonstration that LTP might be indeed the right candidate came from Richard Morris at the University of Edinburgh, whose memory model is conceptually similar to the Barnes maze and became so popular that within the past ten years it has virtually dominated all other memory tests in most psychology labs. The test is simply known as the Morris maze, and is based on rats or mice (or even gerbils) swimming through a cloudy pool of milky water (Figure 9b). The pool contains a small platform just below water level, invisible because of the opacity of the water. A swimming rat first finds the platform by trial and error, and then locates it through memory – just like rats in the Barnes maze – using learned spatial cues in the room. Such spatial memory is believed to require an intact hippocampus.

First, Morris showed that a drug called AP5 (aminophos-phonovaleric acid, sometimes also known as APV) which poisons the crucial NMDA receptors on the recipient cell also blocks the induction of LTP. Next, he wondered, if AP5 reached the hippocampus of the brain of an experimental rat, would it have any effect on spatial memory? So he delivered AP5 to the hippocampus and repeated the swimming test. The drug-injected rats were unable to find the platform: the same drug that blocked LTP retarded spatial memory as well. Morris's experiment lends support to the hypothesis that LTP is a cellular phenomenon that has something to do with learning and memory in the awake and active animal.[26]

There is, however, a piece of the LTP jigsaw missing: LTP has not been seen in an active animal as a result of natural stimulation without the aid of electrical stimulation from the experimenter. Moreover, it increasingly appears that LTP-like phenomena are not restricted to the hippocampus: many other brain areas are susceptible to LTP, including the cerebral cortex, amygdala and striatum. Such evidence, it seems to me, supports LTP as a prime memory storage candidate on the one hand, but on the other, casts some doubt on the drawing of parallels between LTP and memory. Should memories as diverse as the place that we visited and a snake that scared us, subserved, as I described in the previous chapters, by distinct brain structures such as the hippocampus and the amygdala, be maintained by the same LTP machinery? 'Why not?' says Phillip Bradley, a neurobiologist from the University of Newcastle upon Tyne, who studies LTP in young chicks. 'Each memory is a property of the system in which it is stored whereas the storage mechanism is a property of the units of the system. It is like the children's building toy Lego in which all the bricks fit together using the same simple mechanisms but can be assembled into structures ranging from replicas of the Empire State Building to dinosaurs.' Such enthusiasm, for sure, is encouraging; however, as was thoughtfully cautioned by Bliss and Lomo in their original report,

> Whether or not the intact animal makes use in real life of a property which has been revealed by synchronous, repetitive volleys to a population of fibers, the normal patterns of activity along which are unknown, is another matter.

Emotional LTP

The features of long-term potentiation that make it so attractive as a cellular mechanism for declarative memory seem to underlie emotional learning as well.

Fear conditioning has much to offer our understanding of how synaptic alterations during LTP relate to learning and memory. As I mentioned earlier in this chapter, the simultaneous arrival – convergence – of conditioned stimulus and unconditioned stimulus into a common post-synaptic neuron is believed to underlie classical fear conditioning. Fear conditioning therefore is similar to the associative form of LTP, in which the convergence of two inputs, one weak and one strong, on recipient cells grants the weak input the capacity to activate these cells. Could it be that we have emotional LTP for emotional learning?

A set of 'emotional' synapses that use the excitatory amino acid glutamate have been identified in the fear-conditioning pathways – the thalamic cells, the lateral nucleus of the amygdala and cortical projections to the amygdala all appear to contain plenty of glutamate. Because glutamate is important for both hippocampal LTP and memory formation, higher amounts of it in the fear learning pathway suggested this pathway should show LTP. Indeed, LTP does happen in the fear-conditioning pathways: it can be induced in the thalamo–amygdala pathway, the emergency route that helps us to respond to danger instantly. It can also be induced in a cortical projection to the amygdala – the longer pathway that offers a more accurate and thoughtful plan of what to do. What is more, blocking NMDA receptors in the amygdala can obstruct both LTP and fear conditioning. But these findings were made *in vitro*, in chopped slices of amygdala, floating in oxygenated solutions in Petri dishes. In contrast, fear conditioning is a feature of a scared, living animal with all its complex behavioural repertoire. The causal relationship between LTP and emotional learning is nothing but speculative.

And so the question remained: is LTP required during emotional learning? To address this question, Michael Rogan, in LeDoux's laboratory in 1997, and now my colleague at Columbia, probed freely moving rats. He anaesthetized rats, implanted a thin stainless-steel recording electrode into the lateral amygdala, fixed it to the skull with dental cement, and let the rats recover for a few days. He then monitored the electrical properties of the neurons from the scared rats' amygdalae: the extracellular potential in the 'fear centre' was recorded in response to conditioned tones (auditory-evoked potential) while a rat was trained. Increases in such potentials, Rogan and LeDoux had previously shown, are identical to those elicited by electrical induction of LTP in the 'fear path'.[27]

As the tone and shock were paired, and the animal learned to respond to the tone with all the peculiar signs of fear, the electrical response in the amygdala to the tone also grew and remained at a high level. When, however, the tone was repeatedly presented alone and the fear conditioning finally disappeared, the electrical responses from the amygdala were back to normal too. These findings suggest that there is a change in the pathway that processes the conditioned stimulus as the animals learn to associate the sound of the tone with a fearful event. On the basis of this evidence Rogan and LeDoux proposed that critical changes occurred at the synapses in the lateral amygdala. This conclusion was further strengthened by *in vitro* findings of enhanced LTP in slices of the lateral amygdala from fear-conditioned rats. For emotional learning, *emotional LTP* was uncovered.

The LTP-memory camp enthusiastically welcomed 'emotional' LTP. 'Is the LTP-memory connection – at least for one form of learning – now established enough to silence the sceptics?' asked LTP experts Robert Malenka and Roger Nicoll when commenting on the findings in *Nature* in 1997. They gave a similar answer to the one that Bliss and Lomo gave in 1973: 'It remains to be shown that the mechanisms responsible for the behaviourally induced synaptic changes are the same as those underlying electrically induced LTP.' And yet, more and more findings indicate that the enthusiastic studies of LTP have not simply been intellectual games, and that progress continues towards a comprehensive understanding of this attractive mechanism of memory. As one of my ex-colleagues commented when we visited Tim Bliss's lab at the Medical Research Council, London, for the first time ten years ago: 'If it will, indeed, be proven that LTP is the mechanism for learning or memory, Tim should get his Nobel.'

Chapter 7

What Have Genes Got to Do With It?

Whenever science makes a discovery, the devil grabs it while the angels are debating the best way to use it.
Alan Valentine

Finally I have arrived at my 'own' chapter. Everything I am going to tell you in the next few pages will be about genes and memory, although there is no way I can tell you everything there is to know. What I do intend to do is to combine the newest research findings on genes and memory and to give you a flavour of the topic as an 'insider', a scientist who for the past several years has been lucky to work with many talented and ambitious researchers, all of whom, separately or together, are hunting for memory genes in the hope of finding a master switch for memory.

You may wonder what genes have to do with memory. Memory is our life – recalling our childhood, picking up an old photo and reliving a time spent with a friend ten years ago, recognizing a favourite singer's voice on the radio or an admired actor's face on the screen, recalling a story read in elementary school or the names of the football players who won the World Cup in 1994. We do not inherit all these memories from our parents through genes, nor will we transfer them to future generations through genes. And yet genes do affect, at least to some degree, our capacity to learn, to remember and to forget.

How did I get into the gene–memory enterprise? This is

how I remember it, even though I can't be sure which genes exactly contributed to my memory. In January 1992 I was working as a visiting scientist at the Rudolf Magnus Institute, Utrecht, in the Netherlands. I was not there to hunt for memory genes, nor was I expecting to make any great discovery. My aim was more modest: to learn certain biochemical techniques, to characterize some of the biochemical properties of presynaptic proteins called neurogranin and B50, both thought to be involved in memory mechanisms. I was then to go back home and apply my biochemical expertise to memory research on chicks. One day while I was doing a routine experimental procedure, a colleague who had just returned from a trip to the USA said to me, 'You know, Rusiko, I heard that in MIT they have genetically engineered a mouse with a deletion in a specific gene [this is called gene knockout] which does not show long-term potentiation and does not learn anything.'

'How come?' I asked. 'If it doesn't learn anything, how can it survive?'

'Well,' he answered, 'that's all that I heard.'

Six months later, the mice without LTP and learning – αCaMKII mutant mice – became known among memory and LTP researchers simply as Alcino's mice. In July 1992, Alcino Silva, at that time a post-doctoral fellow in Nobel prizewinner Susumu Tonegawa's lab at the Massachusetts Institute of Technology in Boston, published two articles in *Science*.[1] In one of them, Silva and colleagues described the type of molecular-genetic techniques they used to generate the poor dumb creatures, and how the wiring of the brain and its physiology had changed as a result of such molecular manipulations. In another, the researchers reported what actually happened to the mutants' behaviour, which sort of mazes they passed successfully and which they failed. I will come back to Alcino's mice later, but for now I want to tell you the rest of the story. That day in Utrecht, I continued doing my biochemical experiments – pouring the proteins from one tube to another, mixing them with other chemical compounds, spinning them on centrifuges (equipment similar in principle to the domestic drying machine) or loading electrophoresis gels (something like the jelly we have for dessert, but not edible) without ever thinking, planning or even suspecting that the little mouse my Dutch colleague mentioned would be the first mutant I would work with.

Three months after the appearance of the news in *Science*, I was on my way to Cold Spring Harbor Laboratory for an interview with Silva. The silent beauty of the world's most famous village of Science, the smell and colour of the autumn leaves and the feeling of the crisp air charmed me immediately. The lab's excellence and academic reputation do not need my words of endorsement – the world's best scientists and science writers have praised them for over a century. I wanted to work there! But first I had to pass an interview, and in fact it was my very first one. I had no idea what it was that I was supposed to do, why I had to meet with five principal investigators and spend an hour or so with each of them, if I was not going to work with any of them directly, or why I was scheduled to go for a dinner together with Silva and Tim Tully at 7 p.m. when I actually wanted to have dinner with my husband. In the former Soviet Union we never had anything like this, and the novelty of the procedure, which I was anxious to pass successfully, was making me uncomfortable. In addition, even though the Laboratory had hired a few excellent molecular biologists from Russia before me, the view at that time was still that all Russians had a 'weird background' (meaning that graduates from the former Soviet Union might be not qualified to meet American standards in science).

I was stressed and nervous. That I was in the celebrated Cold Spring Harbor Laboratory was alone enough of a scientific shock for me. I was even more galvanized when during lunch Alcino briefly introduced me to one of the world's most renowned Nobel prizewinners and ex-director of the Laboratory, Jim Watson. 'Rusiko is interviewing for a post-doctoral position with me,' Alcino said. Watson, of course, could not care less. His concern was to recruit the best heads of research; it was then up to them whom they wanted to have in their own labs. But I also remember being confident – confident of what I knew, what I wanted, what I was capable of offering. With that in mind, I went through an interview routine: I talked to Alcino about what I did in the past and what I wanted to do in the near future, gave a seminar in the Beckman building,[2] met and talked with other people, and finally, overwhelmed and hungry, went for dinner.

The dinner was a continuation of the interview but in an informal setting: during the five hours, Tully, who was recruited by Jim Watson to lead research on genes controlling learning and memory in the fruit fly *Drosophila*, squeezed the last juices from me by asking what exactly I wanted to do with Alcino's mice, why and how (obviously he wanted to determine whether his friend was getting a good post-doc or not). I was exhausted after a long day, but I enjoyed the scientific exchange immensely. For me, their infectious enthusiasm added fuel to the fire. I thought: 'That's where the future of memory science is, those are the right scientists to work with and that's where I want to be.' I did not say any of this.

A week later, on 10 November 1992, I joined Silva's lab. Perhaps 'joined' is a bit of an exaggeration, because there was not much to join. Apart from Alcino and a newly hired molecular biological technician, Chuan Min Chen, there was one large room with virtually nothing in it but clean, empty benches and shelves waiting for molecular tools and toys to arrive, and another room sixteen metres square – designated for behavioural experiments – containing a big can of white paint, a brush, a ladder and a messy floor, waiting for a painter to finish the job. But importantly there were several 'boy–girl' pairs of mice: some mutants, some normal mice without mutation (wild-types) and some 'mixtures', set aside in the mouse cages for breeding, in a barn-like animal facility. Some of them had already had sex and even managed to produce new generations of mutants and normals, while others were still trying to do their best.

The day after my arrival, I went to the lab early in the morning and did not return home until early in the morning the next day. And this, I must say, became pretty much my daily working routine. In fact, most of my colleagues, Alcino included, had a similarly crazy lifestyle. There was a tremendous amount to do: to decide which projects to pursue first and which could wait for a while, what learning tasks were the best and why, what mazes to buy and from whom, which mice to start the first experiments with, how to use the space properly, which statistical programs to instal on the computers, which software was better and why, and so on and on. In addition, my interests extended beyond behaviour and I began ordering various tools and chemicals to enable me to do some essential neuroanatomical and biochemical work. I was putting everything on 'rush order', one more advantage of Cold Spring Harbor Laboratory: there is virtually no bureaucratic work. If you argue well enough what you need and why, and if what you need is best for your science, you can get it done almost at once. Alcino told me: 'Buy the best of everything,' and he was right: we were building up a new lab and we needed a strong foundation.

Nowadays, laboratories that for years had worked on memory problems in monkeys, rabbits, rats, flies or sea snails have found themselves purchasing water mazes and conditioning chambers for studying genes and memory in mice. But back then in November 1992, when most scientists were sceptical – not to say hostile – about the scientific application of genetically engineered mice to memory research, we were setting up the first behavioural facilities exclusively for probing learning and memory capacities in gene knockouts. More importantly, we were establishing a new branch of memory research, commonly referred to today as 'mouse knockouts and learning', which has since become one of the most popular and dominant fields in neuroscience. Here it is time to turn to a consideration of what the genetically engineered mice actually are and why they are useful for our understanding of the biology of memory.

Knocking Out

Just as the discovery of a common genetic molecule, DNA, shows that all living creatures are linked to each other through long-lost common ancestors, so the modern molecular genetic tools developed to manipulate DNA allow genes to be rearranged into combinations never seen in any ancestral organism. In 1989, Mario Capecci at the University of Utah published an article in which he described a new technique for altering the mouse genome by gene targeting (gene knockout).[3,4] Capecci, whose scientific career began in Jim Watson's lab, dedicated his article to his mentor's sixtieth birthday.

Gene targeting belongs to a set of techniques commonly called reverse genetics. Reverse genetics, in which mutations are produced by replacement of a gene of choice, allow one to deduce the behaviour and physical characteristics of an organism from its genes. The experimenter can choose both which gene to mutate and how to mutate it. The criteria for selecting which gene to mutate can be based on knowledge generated within the species or from other species. Reverse genetic approaches have been used extensively to study development in the mouse, but their use in the study of mouse memory began only in the 1990s. Most mouse genetic techniques that are used today in memory research trace their conceptual and experimental roots back to the genetic study of behaviour in *Drosophila*. They were pioneered at the end of the 1960s by the American geneticist Seymour Benzer and his students, Jeff Hall, Chip Quinn, Yadin Dudai and others at the California Institute of Technology.[5]

Mouse gene targeting is a time-consuming procedure. On average, the generation of a 'knockout' mouse takes about two years – if you are lucky and all stages go smoothly, and you work hard enough. In its simple version, the procedure has four main steps.[6] The first step involves the engineering of the desired mutation into a cloned copy of the chosen gene. The mutated DNA is then transferred into embryonic stem cells using a brief high-voltage electric shock, which creates temporary pores in the cells and allows the mutated DNA to reach the nucleus. It is in the nucleus that the crucial swap happens: the mutant DNA will either replace the 'targeted' gene in a process called homologous recombination, or it might integrate at some irrelevant chromosomal location. In the latter case, consider yourself unlucky and start again. If, however, things go well, you will collect the mutant cells – those that have the normal gene knocked out. These cells are then packaged into a tiny glass pipette and pumped into mouse embryos to generate chimaeras – pretty, black-yellowish striped 'tiger' mice that carry roughly 80 per cent of mutant cells. Next the 'tiger' mouse mates with a normal one to produce mice with a single mutant copy of the gene (heterozygous mice). And finally these offspring mate to produce the long-expected mutants – mice having two mutant copies of the gene (homozygous mice). Wild-types (mice with the normal gene) are also born along with mutants. All brothers and sisters, mutants and normal, grow up together with their parents until about three weeks of age. Thereafter, the 'teens' leave the parental home: the pups are weaned, and 'boys' and 'girls' are separated and placed in gangs of three or four mice per cage until the day comes to recruit them in experiments.

Silva and colleagues employed Capecci's technique to look at how the loss of the αCaMKII gene affects learned behaviour. There were good reasons for the specific interest in this particular gene. First, it is abundant in brain structures primarily concerned with memory. Second, some pharmacological agents that blocked the induction of hippocampal LTP seem to do so through suppression of the function of the αCaMKII gene. Indeed, analysis of knockouts revealed two principal findings. First, αCaMKII appears to be important for the establishment of LTP. Second, the fact that mutants are deficient in both LTP and spatial learning suggests that these two processes are intimately related.

Around the same time as Silva and co-workers were probing their mice, Seth Grant, Eric Kandel and colleagues at Columbia University turned their attention from *Aplysia* to knockout mice. The Columbia researchers received a big shipment of mice lacking a gene called *Fyn* – a key member of the tyrosine kinase family – from Philippe Soriano's lab at Baylor College. They tested the mice and found that like the αCaMKII mutants, *Fyn* knockouts also lacked LTP and spatial learning.[7]

This new branch of mouse genetics offers several advantages

in the molecular study of learning and memory. First, there is an advantage to working with an engineered mutation in a cloned gene rather than a mutation in an unknown gene that occurs naturally or is elicited by chemicals, radiation and so on. Knowledge about the disrupted protein, such as its pattern of expression and biochemical peculiarities, gives solid ground for the interpretation of changes in behaviour. Second, the function of the identified protein can be studied by creating various mutations in the same gene. For example, 'point' mutations can be created, which change only one property of a protein. In short, this sophisticated procedure involves substitution of a normal single amino acid with a mutated one in a functionally critical part of the protein. These in turn may produce only subtle alterations in neuronal physiology and memory processes. Third, one can manipulate distinct subtypes of the same receptor, for which specific pharmacological agents may not be available and so the role of these receptors in memory formation cannot be studied. And finally, once created, virtually unlimited quantities of mutants can be produced with identical and precise genetic manipulations. A substantial benefit is that one can then investigate the impact of these genetic mutations on the relationship between different aspects of neuronal function and memory. So the very same animal can be used to study the link: genes → cells → neural networks → mind.

However, the engineered mice – no matter how dull or clever – are not without problems. Indeed, there has been much heated discussion about their usefulness. The brain – a mouse's, yours or mine – is an extraordinarily plastic structure and organisms have unique adaptive capacities. So one potential problem is that sometimes the function of the deleted gene can be compensated for, partially or even completely, throughout development. This will either mask or complicate the interpretation of changes in behaviour. Another major concern is that genetic manipulation often produces more than one effect on behaviour.

I'll discuss some of the recent technological advances in mouse genetics that have enhanced the power of this approach later in the chapter, but for the moment let me share with you some of the concerns and thoughts that I came across when studying memory.

A Few Thoughts from a Mouse Veteran

No amount of experimentation can ever prove me right; a single experiment can prove me wrong. *Albert Einstein*

He had read Shakespeare and found him weak in chemistry.
H. G. Wells

Molecular genetic and cellular studies obviously deserve the highest credit, but one has to keep in mind that the ultimate function of the nervous system is to initiate, maintain and adjust behaviour. It is the behaviour we express through memory, and memory we express through behaviour, that concern us the most.

Over the past few years I have often received telephone calls from young molecular biologists, most of them asking the same question: 'I generated such-and-such a knockout and I want to test its learning and memory. Could you tell me what I should do?' There is nothing wrong with such questions and I always welcome them. What is wrong, however, is the naive expectation that one can actually learn how to study animal learning and memory over the telephone.

The measurement of behaviour is often considered the 'easy' part of an experiment. Right and wrong! Certainly, it is relatively easy to measure the number of errors a mouse makes in a maze or the time it takes to find an escape platform in a cloudy water pool. However, the ease of making this kind of behavioural measure is misleading, for at least three reasons. First, the interpretation of these measures is a complicated process; second, it is not easy to determine if what we are measuring are the proper parameters of behaviour or (even more importantly) if we are indeed probing appropriate behaviours; and third, it is difficult to design an experiment with the sufficient and necessary behavioural controls.

As with everything else, genes do not work in a vacuum. Any one of many genes can disrupt development, but the normal range of behavioural variation is likely to be orchestrated by a system of many genes, each with a small effect, as well as by environmental influences. I have already mentioned that most genes are likely to have multiple affects on behaviour and that behaviour is likely to be influenced by many genes. This complexity makes it improbable that a simple pathway exists between genes and memory. As a result, it is often difficult to predict what sort of learning might be altered by manipulation of a given gene, and which memory will be lost, which will be intact or which will perhaps even be upgraded.

With these thoughts in mind, I set a few rules for my memory research at Cold Spring Harbor, which since then I have tried to follow.

Rule One: *Make sure that observed changes in learning and/or memory are not merely non-specific effects of a gene alteration to the brain. Therefore, demonstrate that different neural substrates are functionally dissociable with the tests chosen*

What does this mean and how does one do this? As I described early in the book, there is now convincing evidence

that declarative and non-declarative memories are subserved
by different brain structures. The former requires the hippocampus, whereas the latter does not. Mice, of course, can't
declare, 'That's what I remember, and that's what I forgot.'
But as happens in humans, the mice with hippocampal
lesions learn and remember some simple puzzles, but fail on
more complex tasks. Take, for example, the Morris water-
maze task I described in Chapter 6. When placed into a pool,
mice without the hippocampus can easily learn to find an
escape platform if it is marked by some sort of cue (such as a
small golfball). The puzzle is called the visible-platform task.
These mice, however, lose their way completely if the safe
platform is no longer marked by a cue and the platform is
hidden under milky water. This is called a hidden-platform or
spatial version of the water task. In this instance, all that is
left for a mouse to rely on are the visual cues surrounding the
pool, and, on the basis of these cues, it forms a mental map of
the environment. And that is precisely what is beyond the
mental capacity of hippocampus-damaged animals. Their
companions with an intact hippocampus have no difficulty
in solving such problems.

So if you suspect that the gene manipulation has affected
the proper functioning of hippocampus-dependent memory,
you have to probe your mouse on both versions of the pool
task. If your mutant mice can't master the simple version of
the pool game as well as their non-mutant friends, the
chances are, first, that your mice may not even see a marked
platform; second, that they can see but can't swim well;
third, they are not motivated to swim and to find the platform, they simply do not care, or they are helpless; fourth,
they are too stressed and anxious, and that's why they fail; or
fifth – none of the above, but the mice are so stupid that they
cannot even learn the simple association between the visible

cue and a safe place. It is then up to you to work out whether you are dealing with 'non-specific' effects or a mouse's failure to learn and remember a simple puzzle.

Rule Two: *To ensure that the experiments are really measuring a particular memory capacity, study subjects on multiple tests of the same inferred capacity*

Say you want to study the impact of a lost gene on spatial memory. You run your mice on the spatial version of the pool task and you see poor memory. You are happy, your work was rewarded! The mice you generated (or a collaborator gave you to test) have a spatial memory loss, you believe. But you now run the mice in the Barnes circular maze – a labyrinth that taxes spatial memory capacity in the same manner as does the water pool – and surprisingly, perhaps even disappointingly, you find no differences between your mutants and normal mice. You are puzzled as to what has happened: why did the memory deficit disappear? How do you explain this? Maybe the gene you modified has nothing to do with spatial memory? Maybe the two tasks place on mutants different motivational or perceptional demands, even though both require spatial memory talent? Maybe your experimental room or equipment is not properly set to evaluate spatial memory? The possibilities are endless, and you have to sweat for hundreds of hours to figure out *where*, *when* and *why* things went wrong, before making any valid conclusions.

Rule Three: *A detailed knowledge of the natural history of behaviour is crucial*

Why? You think: I work in an artificial laboratory environment, not in a field, and there are many standardized memory tasks available. But say you want to modify some memory test. Then you have to consider the following fact:

mice that came into your experiment already have a well-established (natural) behavioural repertoire. The knowledge of this repertoire might be essential to understanding the results of an experiment, while lack of such knowledge can often lead to experiments that are quite unsuitable to answer the question for which they were conceived.

Rule Four: *Assessment of several measurements and detailed analysis of the motor patterns acquired by an animal will give a much more precise indication than a single measure of whether or not memory was actually stored*

Let me give you an example. There is a simple task called 'step-down', which is used for testing a mouse's fear memory. In this task, a mouse is placed on a small pedestal in the middle of the conditioning chamber. As soon as it steps down, it gets a brief tingle of electricity to its feet through a grid floor. Whenever a mouse is next placed on the pedestal, it remembers the unpleasant event and prefers to stay there instead of stepping down onto the nasty floor. What is usually measured in this test is the time a mouse takes to step down. If, say, the time is long, then it is claimed that the mouse has a 'good memory'. If, however, the mouse steps down soon, it is considered to have a 'bad memory'. On the basis of this measure, you can divide mice into two groups: one group with good memory, and the other with a bad memory. But sometimes, if you watch a mouse for a few more seconds after it has stepped down onto the grid floor, surprisingly, you will find out that what you scored as bad memory, solely by taking only one measure, is actually not true. The mouse tagged with 'bad memory' will be standing frozen, scared, in expectation of the unpleasant event. If you now score the time it spends frozen (freezing usually means complete immobility with the exception of breathing), you will have to give it credit for remembering the fearful event that had happened the day before.

Rule Five: *There is no memory without learning – there is learning without memory*

I will come back to this when I describe genes important for long-term memory, but for the moment I want to go back to those 'learning' mutants that remind me of the 'village of science'.

The Inauguration of the Pool

As the rules were established and equipment set up, we began the first set of experiments. The inauguration of the pool (on Christmas Day, 1992) was done with mutant mice carrying a single copy of the αCaMKII gene. At first glance, the mice looked healthy, cheerful and much like their normal siblings. If knocking out the αCaMKII gene produced a complete 'spatial learning and LTP invalid', we wondered, what would be the impact of the loss of a half of this gene product – αCaMKII protein – on learning? We took a whole family of αCaMKII mice – heterozygous, homozygous and wild-types – to compete against each other in learning tasks.

As we suspected, αCaMKII heterozygous mice won second place – they were inferior to their wild-type competitors but superior to homozygous mice. For example, they behaved poorly in the spatial version of the water maze – a task that is sensitive to hippocampal lesions. However, they mastered the visible-platform version of the pool game – the one not affected by hippocampal damage. So far, you may be thinking that this sounds like the results reported by Silva and collaborators for αCaMKII homozygous mice. Where is the superiority? What did they do that was so special? First, our half-mutants, when trained more extensively, were able to compensate for the spatial learning deficit, while full mutants were not. Second, despite the fact that the full mutants could swim and see, they appeared much slower than the half-mutants in learning the visible platform task; and this, as I mentioned above, is not a good sign. It points out that the deletion of the entire gene produced some sort of non-specific effects that confound the interpretation of a spatial memory deficit.

The next round of competition took place in fear conditioning chambers. In the fear conditioning task a mouse learns at least two things: to fear a neutral sound (cued conditioning) and to fear a chamber (context conditioning). In addition to all the advantages of fear conditioning that I described earlier, this relatively simple puzzle allows the dissociation of two types of memory. Remembering context is highly dependent on the proper functioning of the hippocampus, while remembering a tone is not. Memories of both, however, will be wiped out if the central executor of emotional learning, the amygdala, is damaged.

What we found was surprising. Not only did our mutants have problems in the cognitively challenging spatial memory task, but they had problems in emotional learning as well: mice showed no hint of contextual fear. But as in the pool task, the half-mutants could compensate for the contextual learning deficits with additional practice, whilst full mutants could not. The half-mutants also showed evidence of being conditioned to a tone while their full mutant companions failed on that task as well. Our experiments clearly indicated that it was the loss of all the αCaMKII protein, not just half of it, that created an irreversible deficit in the learning capacities of the mice, and this deficit obviously extended beyond memory tasks that need the hippocampus. In contrast, learning disabilities of mice carrying only a single copy of the αCaMKII gene were mild and were largely compensated for by additional training.[8] These mice were just slow learners.

So far, so good. But what sort of synaptic processes could possibly explain their behaviour? That was up to physiologists to find out. Paul Chapman, who came from the University of Minnesota, Minneapolis, to do his summer sabbatical with us, and Bruno Franguelli, who arrived from the UK for post-doctoral training, began extensive investigation of physiological processes in hippocampal slices of the half-mutants. Amazingly, these mice appeared to have normal LTP in the CA1 region of the hippocampus. Abnormalities were, however, identified in the function of 'short-lived' plasticity (changes in synaptic strength that last from milliseconds to seconds). Perhaps abnormal short-lived plasticity on the one hand, but normal LTP on the other even with poor hippocampus-dependent learning, can explain why our half-mutants could substantially compensate for the learning deficit with additional training. Although such a possibility seemed attractive, especially because in some organisms short-lived changes in synapses might endow neural circuits with the ability to adapt quickly to changing environments, we needed some additional experimental proof.

Luckily, Thomas Sudhof and colleagues at the University of Texas Southwestern Medical School, Dallas, generated mice with mutations that could address our question. These were knockouts that lacked the key proteins synapsin I and synapsin II. These proteins are activated by αCaMKII kinase and so serve as molecular substrates for it. If, we thought, there are indeed links between αCaMKII kinase, short-lived plasticity and learning, then mice lacking the αCaMKII substrates should be pretty similar to our half-mutants. This proved to be the case.

Thomas Sudhof, who came to the Cold Spring Harbor Laboratory to give a seminar, reported that both knockouts had a deficit in short-lived plasticity but apparently normal LTP. What else could we have wished for at that time? The collaboration started immediately and the mice were shipped from Dallas. Texan mice behaved much like their Long Island cousins: they, too, had a learning deficit, but they, too, with more rehearsal, were able to overcome it. Perhaps normal LTP was helpful in compensating for their gloominess.

Knocking Sometimes

The early gene-targeting studies of learning and memory were based on mice with complete or partial deletions of chosen genes. To test a specific hypothesis, however, it is often very useful to alter only certain small pieces of an otherwise intact gene. So to further tease apart the role of αCaMKII in learning and in the physiological properties of neuronal cells, Karl Peter Giese, a molecular biologist who joined the lab shortly after me, generated a mouse with a point mutation.

The CaMKII has one exquisite property to enable it to act as a molecular switch for memory. When calcium levels increase in a cell, this kinase undergoes a biochemical process called autophosphorylation – switching itself from an inactive to a permanently active state. To do this, the molecule has a special dispatcher, an amino acid, threonine 286 (Thr-286). Once the dispatcher receives a signal that the level of calcium is increased, the button is pressed and autophosphorylation is initiated: the CaMKII becomes biochemically greedy, trapping a thousand times more calcium–calmodulin all at once. Such 'savings' then allow the molecule to remain activated for minutes or even hours without any further need for high calcium–calmodulin levels. If, however, Thr-286 is substituted by another amino acid called alanine, the capacity of this kinase to be persistently active is shut off. It was this quality of CaMKII that attracted Giese's and Silva's attention. What would happen to learning if this unique inborn capacity of the molecule were blocked?

Giese introduced the alanine mutant into embryonic stem cells to generate new mice.[9] As suspected, persistent activation of the kinase indeed appeared to be crucial for hippocampal cell communication. These mutant mice, stripped of their unique biochemical property, acted as dumb as the mice with complete deletion of the CaMKII gene: mice lost their way in the spatial maze even after many training trials. When the hippocampal slices were studied for the existence of LTP, the slices from the mutants did not show it. To make the story complete, the mice were tested for their capacity to form and maintain hippocampal place cells. The function of place cells, as I described earlier, is to encode information about place. By doing so, place cells help the animal to form a spatial map of its surroundings. Place cells are established within minutes, and, once established, the spatial map to which they contribute can remain stable for hours and weeks. Does the lack of LTP affect in some ways the formation or maintenance of place cells? Do genetic manipulations that interfere with LTP and spatial learning capacity do so by interfering with place cells? Although the causal relationship between spatial learning, LTP and place cells is not established, studies gave some initial hints. It seems that it is the stability of place cells, but not their initial formation, which is affected by the absence of LTP.

Another set of elegant findings that pointed out the importance of the hippocampal LTP and the stability of place cells in
spatial memory has come from studies of mice that have
region-specific gene disruption. In 1996, Tonegawa's group at
MIT selectively knocked out one subunit of the NMDA receptor in the neurons of the CA1 region. Such precise and restricted gene manipulation produced mice with a striking deficit in
LTP in the CA1 region, spatial memory, and the ability to
maintain place cells.[10] Thus, the chain linking genes, LTP,
place cells and spatial memory was strengthened once again.

Nonetheless, targeted knockouts, no matter how well
restricted, have a potential problem. Because the gene is
absent throughout development, the deficit in spatial
memory could be caused by some developmental defect such
as abnormal wiring of hippocampal nerve cells. To address
this problem, Mark Mayford, in 1996 my colleague at
Columbia, now at the University of California, San Diego, La
Jolla, developed yet another molecular genetic technique. To
gain control over genes, Mark Mayford and Eric Kandel generated a new type of mutant mouse, called an inducible transgenic, in which the mutated gene can be switched on and off
by adding to the mouse's food or water a commonly used,
bitter-tasting antibiotic, tetracycline.[11] Instead of knocking
out the αCaMKII gene, these researchers added the αCaMKII
transgene, a mutated form of this gene, throughout the hippocampus and other neighbouring structures involved in
memory. This manipulation, as expected, interfered with
LTP, the stability of place cells and spatial learning.
However, the defects caused by the mutation seemed to
disappear when mice were fed with antibiotic and the
expression of the transgene was shut off.

The implication of these findings is extraordinary: not only
do they strengthen the link between LTP, place cells and

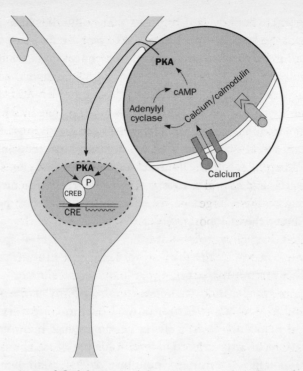

Figure 10 A simplified diagram of the cAMP cascade (other molecules activate CREB)

spatial memory, but they also hold out the possibility of the manipulation of gene function with drugs. The tetracycline-regulated system has now been combined with the technique of producing region-specific mutations. This will allow us to control both *when* and *where* in the brain the gene of interest is turned on and off.

Protein Synthesis, cAMP and CREB

The stakes in the memory gene venture rose considerably during the 1960s and 1970s when several scientists made an intriguing observation. New proteins, synthesized within neurons during learning, appeared to be essential raw material for long-term memory, just as bricks are used to construct a house. But the significance of this goes beyond the trivial notion that neurons, like other cells, require protein synthesis for survival. If you give animals a drug that blocks their ability to make new proteins, they become incapable of forming long-lasting memories. They can learn, and they can even keep in mind the learned task for an hour or so. But check their memory five or six hours later, or the next day, and you will be surprised by their stupidity – they have no clue about the task whatsoever.

What happened to the memory? Where did it go? The answer is nowhere: the drug simply prevented the conversion of short-term memory into long-term memory. This mechanistic distinction between short-term memory and long-term memory – formation of long-term memory needs new proteins, while formation of short-term memory does not – is apparently universal and holds up for all creatures so far studied in laboratories, including *Aplysia*, fish, fruit flies, bees, chicks, mice, rats and rabbits. The implications are profound: since genes must be switched to make new proteins, they are, therefore, involved in long-term memory. What are these genes and what triggers them?

Back in Cold Spring Harbor, when we started hunting for genes involved in laying down long-term memories in mice, we had a few tentative hints where to search. Some of the earliest molecular events involved in learning in invertebrates are mediated by a molecular signalling system called the cyclic AMP (cAMP) pathway. For example, learning in *Aplysia* is disrupted if this signalling system is perturbed. Similarly, learning disabilities in fruit-fly mutants called *dunce*, *rutabaga*, *amnesiac*, *RIα* and *Gsα* stem from mutations in genes affecting some earlier molecular steps in the cAMP pathway.[12] Two different animals, same pathway. Quite a hint here.

But how does learning trigger cAMP signalling? If I avoid some of the tongue-twisting names of the molecules of the cAMP pathway, a simplified chain would be as depicted in Figure 10. When a cell receives a signal about some learning event, the intracellular concentration of cAMP increases. Cyclic AMP binds to a protein called cAMP-dependent protein kinase A (PKA). This is made up from four smaller proteins (subunits) bound together into one protein complex. As the concentration of cAMP increases, two of the PKA subunits bind cAMP. As a result, PKA changes its shape and frees two active (catalytic) components of the kinase. These liberated proteins move to the nucleus where they activate a molecule known as a cAMP-response element binding protein, CREB. Activated CREB then binds to its designated sites on DNA, called cAMP-response elements (CRE-elements), and switches on dozens of other genes.

If the model is correct, and the chain works properly, the end result is synthesis of new proteins – the necessary 'bricks' that, inserted here and there, strengthen the connectivity between synapses to form memories. If so, and CREB dictates whether or not a cell will make new proteins in response to cAMP signalling, then perhaps CREB is the key to long-term memory?

In 1990, Pramo Dash and Eric Kandel injected a 'cocktail' of molecules containing artificially prepared CREs into a neural cell preparation isolated from *Aplysia* and studied the synaptic response.[13] While the cocktail did not affect short-term changes in neurotransmitter release (short-term facilitation), it completely blocked long-term strengthening of synaptic connections (also called long-term facilitation). The Columbia

University researchers reasoned that the injected CRE competitors prevented internal CREBs from binding to DNA because they occupied all of the CRE sites. In doing so, they trapped all the CREB molecules, preventing them from doing their job – that is, activating the protein synthesis machinery necessary for long-term facilitation. These findings provided an important hint: CREB seemed to be the gateway to memory's genes. But whether CREB had anything to do with memory in live and active animals awaited work on the fly and mouse.

The Master Switch for Long-term Memory?

Whenever man comes up with a better mousetrap, nature immediately comes up with a better mouse. *James Carswell*

There are several sorts of truth that I could tell about the decade of my work on genes and memory. One would be the version reported at conferences or published in scientific papers. It consists of smooth, logical stories, which always involve a set of well-designed, unambiguous experiments, build on earlier data and theoretical models, point to future directions, and acknowledge the work of colleagues. The second 'truth' would be the version found in the reports in newspapers and popular magazines, with sensational titles such as: 'Scientists Find Gene For Memory' or 'Of Mice, Humans and Genetic Mysteries'.[14] The third version would be the story behind the conferences or scientific papers that reflects the true chronology of the experiments done – who did what, why, when and how.

I will leave aside the second 'truth'. This leaves me with two versions of the same story – the logical and the chronological. Fortunately, they fit well with one another; no matter where I start, I will end up on the same pathway. My only concern is to make the story as readable as possible and so I will mix the two. But what I shall try to avoid is telling you some of the 'scientific intrigues' that are an inevitable part of doing science. These 'intrigues' are mainly about who deserves credit for this or that idea, model or experiment; whose findings are 'clear-cut' and whose are 'fuzzy', whose papers should be published in *Cell* or *Nature* and whose should be trashed; who was just lucky to succeed and who has worked hard for his or her luck. Scientists, as Jim Watson commented in the *New York Times*, 'are like Michael Douglas's characters – a little evil and very competitive' (Watson did not, however, say anything about how female scientists fit this comparison).

It was at the traditional lobster banquet after the annual Cold Spring Harbor Laboratory conference in November 1993 that Tim Tully asked me: 'So, Rusiko, what are you planning to do with CREB knockouts?'

'I want to give them training which will enable me to dissociate learning from memory, so I can see if CREB is exclusively involved in formation of long-term memories or has something to do with learning and short-term memory as well,' I answered.

A few months before this conversation, Alcino learned that cancer researcher Gunter Schutz and his fellow post-docs Edith Hummler, Timothy Cole and Judy Blendy at the University of Heidelberg had genetically engineered a mouse that lacked the CREB gene. A collaboration between Schutz's lab and our lab was arranged and the CREB mice were shipped to Cold Spring Harbor. There was much excitement about the 'CREB arrival', both in our lab and in Tully's lab. Jerry Yin, a molecular biologist in Tully's lab, had some evidence that mutation of the CREB gene affected memory in fruit flies in a rather specific way: flies lacking the CREB gene could not form long-term memory but their short-term memory was perfectly normal.[15] Although promising and exciting, these findings needed further confirmation. As 'fly people' say at Cold Spring Harbor: 'Flies are flies, and mice are people.' The genome of a mouse is virtually identical to the genome of a human; we may not look much alike, but our genes do. Everyone was eagerly awaiting the outcome of the experiments on the CREB mice.

As Tim and Jerry continued their 'Ebbinghaus type' experiments on flies, teaching them with massed or spaced training sessions how to remember a smell associated with a shock, I began running the CREB mice in the mazes. First, I trained them in a Pavlovian conditioning model, which I described in previous chapters. The results were clear-cut. When I tested mice either thirty or sixty minutes after a training session, both normal and CREB mutant mice showed an identical memory for fear: CREB mutants remembered perfectly well the context in which they had an aversive experience and they also remembered that the tone was a predictor of danger. In striking contrast, when CREB mutants were tested two hours or twenty-four hours after training, they showed no hints of fear. Clearly, in mice with a mutant CREB gene, short-term memory remains normal, but long-term memory does not form. Similarly, CREB mutants were much worse than wild-type mice at recalling the location of a platform in a water maze, suggesting that CREB may be a key regulator of spatial memory as well.

Given the importance of the hippocampus in generating long-term memory and the correlation of long-term potentiation in this region of the brain with information storage, the next step was to look at LTP in the CREB mice. So Bruno Franguelli made an *in vitro* comparison of the duration of LTP in hippocampal slices of the CREB-deficient mice with the wild-type mice. Short-term synaptic plasticity (described earlier in the chapter) was identical in the mutant and wild-type animals; but LTP was less in mutants than in normal mice, and it disappeared fast. So the CREB-deficient animals not only had severe deficiency in long-term memory but also had an abnormal long-term synaptic communication.

These findings took about 250 days of intensive work. The conclusion that the CREB gene was important for long-term memory but not for short-term memory or for learning was too serious and too demanding – could it be that the very same gene is critical for long-term memory, but not needed for short-term memory? Is it really so? Although all experiments were done 'blind' – that is, the experimenter did not know which mouse was a mutant and which was a wild-type – they needed to be repeated and reproduced. Diana Cioffi, an undergraduate student, and I divided a new shipment of mice into two groups. She trained one group of mice and I trained the other. Independently we got the same results – CREB mutants had good short-term memory but they could not form long-term memory.[16]

I can't say who was happier on learning about our results – we, the 'mouse people', or our colleagues, the 'fly people'. Tim seemed so excited that the forgetfulness of our CREB mutant mice closely resembled what they saw in fruit flies with a deficient CREB gene that he invited us to celebrate our 'CREB findings'. A few months later, the findings 'Of Mice and Flies' were published side by side as three full-length articles in Cell, and were even highlighted on the cover of the distinguished journal. They were extremely well received by both the scientific and the popular press.

What was so important about these experiments? First, they represent the first genetic demonstration in behaving animals that short-term memory and long-term memory are separate memory systems – the argument I advocated earlier in this book. Second, the similarity in results in fruit flies and mice, together with studies in *Aplysia*, indicated that CREB must be an evolutionarily conserved molecule involved in the switch of short-term memory into long-term memory. As Michael Greenberg, a leading neuroscientist at Harvard Medical School wrote:

> studies in systems ranging from two mollusk neurons in culture to complex behaviours in mammals have revealed a molecular mechanism by which memories are generated... To me, the most striking finding is the involvement of CREB in the process of information storage in a living animal.[17]

One must, however, keep in mind that CREB is present in many other cells of the body besides neurons. It is in fact believed to play a part in hormone metabolism, drug addiction and body clocks.

If it was largely Eric Kandel's work that prompted my work on CREB and memory, it was my work on CREB mutants that brought me to Kandel's lab. Kandel's lifetime devotion to the study of the role of cyclic AMP signalling in memory is a monumental achievement, as Larry Squire says, and I could not agree more. So I reasoned that if I wanted to pursue my interests and study further how cAMP signalling is involved in memory processes, I should join Kandel's group. I did, and I continued my scientific trip along the fascinating cAMP pathway.

When protein kinase A moves to the nucleus it activates CREB. What would happen to memory if PKA were inactivated? Would memory suffer? Ted Abel, Peter Nguyen, Mark Barad, Eric Kandel and I created mutant mice expressing a gene that inhibited the activity of PKA.[18] Like the CREB mutants, these animals showed selective defects in synaptic communications. Early LTP, which lasts only an hour or two, was normal. In contrast, the late phase of LTP, which normally lasts for eight to ten hours and like long-term memory requires protein synthesis, waned within one or two hours. But what about the memory capabilities of these mice?

Studies revealed several important findings. First, as we predicted, disruption of the PKA pathway leads to severe defects in long-term memory whilst short-term memory is good. Second, the deficit is only evident when task-solving requires the hippocampus, but not the amygdala, or a brain area called the gustatory cortex. This latter structure, as advocated by Yadin Dudai of the Weizmann Institute in Jerusalem, is crucial for forming memories about poisoned food (taste aversion). The discrepancy in memorizing different tasks – clearly favouring multiple memory system concepts – was not surprising because in these mutants the PKA pathway was most disrupted in the hippocampus, not in the amygdala or the gustatory cortex. So for short-term memory to be transformed into long-term memory, the pathway leading to the CREB gene must work properly.

Meanwhile, the research on CREB exploded. Reports about the crucial role of CREB in long-term memory and long-lasting neuronal communication began to sprout like mushrooms after rain (Figure 11). One after another, elegant experiments in flies, *Aplysia* and rats revealed that boosting CREB could produce memory akin to photographic memory in humans. New evidence supporting our findings about the role of CREB in spatial memory came from California. There, James McGaugh's team drizzled a special chemical that blocks CREB into the hippocampus of the rat's brain. Like our CREB mice, McGaugh's rats with inactivated CREB lost the ability to form spatial memory. Further south, Ivan

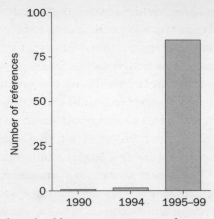

Figure 11 Number of publications on CREB and memory in reviewed journals (data obtained from Medline)

Izquierdo at the Institute of Biology of Porto Alegre in Brazil and Jorge Medina at the University of Buenos Aires in Argentina observed increased amounts of CREB protein in the hippocampus as rats memorized a fearful event in a step-down scheme. Activity of CREB appeared to be crucial for long-lasting memory of a variety of tasks in which rodents have to remember which food is safe to eat and which is not. Finally, there is tempting evidence that CREB malfunction may account for some human mental disorders as well.[19]

As Mark Bear, a neuroscientist at Brown University, has commented, 'the CREB system represents one of the most exciting developments in neurobiology over the past several years, because it seems to operate similarly in a number of different organisms.'[20] Not surprisingly, research into CREB switch has become a matter of not only academic but also commercial urgency as well. In 1997, two 'memory companies' (according to a news release), Helicon Therapeutics and Memory Pharmaceuticals, were formed to search for memory-improving drugs based on the CREB switch.

Yet behind the euphoria that greets each new discovery lurks a nagging sense of dissatisfaction. Exactly how do genes affect neuronal plasticity? In which synapses, and in how many of them, are particular memories stored? Where exactly are the long-term memory cells located, those engrams for which Karl Lashley searched for forty years? How does CREB decide which memories should be stored and which should be ignored? How many genes does CREB target? How many pathways lead to CREB? Is CREB the only molecular switch for memory? And if not, how many more are there?

The truth is that we don't have all the answers yet. But even in the past three years, from the moment I decided to write this book until the moment I am about to finish, we have accumulated colossal findings. They will be filtered and polished; some will be proved and others will be refuted by new evidence. It is a long way to go, but as Eric Kandel likes to put it, 'we do have a nice beginning'. Memory is a mystery whose secrets have been slowly unfolding for years.

Where Do We Go From Here?

If the Human race wants to go to hell in a basket, technology can help it get there by jet. *Charles M. Allen*

I have seen similar headings many times in scientific or popular literature and, I must admit, I don't like them, even though the question is legitimate. Unless one writes about clear future strategy, what is usually summed up beneath these 'goodbye notes' is what has been already said 'between the lines' throughout the text. Sometimes, the notes are so long that one even begins to lose track of where one was to begin with. And I am of the opinion that if you give yourself more time to think, you eventually understand the main message of any story. I will, therefore, be brief.

The molecular genetics of memory will clearly be a major area of research. Yet the conclusions of such research should be tempered with caution. Basic genetic research has taught biologists that genes do not work in a vacuum. Rather, there is complex interaction among many genes. If one further considers the role of the environment in gene expression, the factors involved in such aspects of life as behaviour, personality, emotion, reasoning, thought, learning and memory become immeasurable. 'The "nature versus nurture" debate in biology must be dismissed as oversimplified by contemporary genetic research,' says Tim Tully. Put simply, genes do not *determine* behaviour; rather they influence it in concert with personality and the social environment.

This principle is particularly true when we talk about memory. Memory is what defines who we are and who others are in our own minds. Memory shapes our intellectual and moral personality, the way we think, smile, say hello and behave in day-to-day life. Indeed, it would be impossible to live as one person, with an individual history, or to possess our being in a continuous fashion, without the memory threads that constantly link our present to our past and prospective future. Science may never be able to fathom the complexity of memories, even though we may understand the basic blocks from which memory is made. Memory is what makes it possible for us to *live* but not to *exist*. Genes cannot *determine* memories, but they do affect our capacity to remember and to forget.

So what do I and other scientists ultimately hope to achieve by hunting for 'memory' genes? I cannot, of course, speak for all scientists, but I believe at the heart of what we are trying to do is the hope that we will be able to gain a better understanding of the molecular mechanisms of which memories are made. This, in turn, will allow the development of drug treatments for patients suffering from memory lapses, including the terrible losses caused by diseases such as Alzheimer's, dementia or age-related mental decline. Perhaps the lost memories will never be recovered. But drugs that improve the long-term retention and storage of new information – perhaps as trivial as remembering a new acquaintance's name or telephone number – will emerge, it seems to me, in the foreseeable future. Similarly, effective treatments could be developed to ease the memories of traumatic events, those horrible 'flashbacks' that persist for years or sometimes for life in the victims of war, violent crime, bombs or sexual abuse.

My optimism is based on my memories of what we as humans have achieved in science, medicine and technology over the past few decades. What is more, research on the biology of memory is still very young. These are not my romantic 'goodbye notes', rather they are my true scientific beliefs. But before they will be fulfilled, there will be many disappointments. These disappointments will arise from both the predictable and the unpredictable effects of memory compounds: there will be 'no effects', 'side effects' and even 'lethal effects'. But perhaps the most serious worry about this technology will emerge from the abuse of memory drugs. Probably they will be taken not only by people who need them but also by healthy people who have a perfectly good memory. For example, they might be used and abused by schoolchildren simply to get better grades or to cover a school programme that normally takes four years in one year; or by young adults so that they can boost their mental performance in order to land a better job. This in turn might create at least three problems. Can everyone afford such 'smart' drugs? And if not, would it be fair to those who cannot afford memory drugs and have to work for years to achieve the same performance?

The second problem would be that even though the immediate outcome of such drugs might be a sharpening of memory, in the long run they might have an opposite effect – a dulling of memory. In short, what helps your grandmother might not help you. That should not surprise us. There is no reason to assume that, for most of us at most times, our molecular machinery that produces CREBs, enzymes and neurotransmitters is not working more or less optimally. Normally, the brain is well buffered against the effect of arbitrary increases or decreases in circulating chemicals, and increasing their activity is no guarantee of increased mental performance. And even if it were, an overpowering memory, as brilliantly described by Alexander Luria, might create a social and intellectual misfit like Mr Shereshevsky. People with exceptional, photographic memories often have enormous difficulty making even simple decisions, because at the same time they can think of fifty different options to choose from. Often, there is a great adaptive value in forgetting certain things. It clears the mind and allows us to concentrate on important values and think in perspective, rather than rummaging indefinitely in meaningless details. More does not necessarily mean better. Jorge Luis Borges describes this powerfully when he has the hero of *Funes, 'el Memorioso'* say:

> I have more memories in myself alone than all men have had since the world was a world…my dreams are like your vigils…my memory, sir, is like a garbage disposal.[21]

As with everything else, memory drugs will have pros and cons. The intelligent thing to do with memory drugs will be to use them intelligently. By no means am I reducing our memories to single genes, or for that matter to any other molecules. However, if we are going to intervene pharmaco-logically in order to cure or prevent memory problems, we must know the workings of proteins encoded by memory-related genes and we must know how to change the way they work.

Memories are oceans of things,
Some, splendoured, need to be preserved and cherished,
Others, causing tears and breaking a heart apart,
Better to be forgotten, forgotten, all at once!

Notes and references

Chapter 1

1. Perhaps I realized this most strongly when I visited England for the first time in 1989, to work at the Open University with Steven Rose. At that time, good-quality typing paper was in short supply in the Soviet Union and I was shocked to see how much paper was used for the simple but endless memoranda individually mailed to each member of the department.
2. Quoted in Herrmann, D. J., and Chaffin, R. *Memory in Historical Perspective: The Literature Before Ebbinghaus* (Springer, New York, 1988).
3. For histories about memory scholarship *see* Herrmann, D. J., and Chaffin, R. *Memory in Historical Perspective: The Literature Before Ebbinghaus* (Springer, New York, 1988); Yates, F. A. *The Art of Memory* (The University of Chicago Press, London, 1966); Carruthers, M. J. *The Book of Memory. A Study of Memory in Medieval Culture* (Cambridge University Press, 1990).
4. Cicero, *De Oratore*, II, lxxxvi, 351–360. Quoted in Herrmann, D. J., and Chaffin, R. *Memory in Historical Perspective: The Literature Before Ebbinghaus* p. 78 (Springer, New York, 1988).
5. Cicero, *De Oratore*, II, lxxxvi, 351–354. Quoted in Yates, F. *The Art of Memory* p. 2 (University of Chicago Press, London, 1966).
6. *Rhetorica Ad Herennium*. Quoted in Yates, F. *The Art of Memory* p. 7 (The University of Chicago Press, London, 1966).
7. Quoted in Patten, B. M. The history of memory arts. *Neurobiology* (1990) 40, 346–352.
8. Quoted in Yates, F. *The Art of Memory* p. 23–26 (The University of Chicago Press, London, 1966).

9. Quoted in Yates, F. *The Art of Memory* (The University of Chicago Press, London, 1966).

10. Quoted in Wilson, J. L., and the editors of *Life*. *The Mind* (Time, New York, 1964).

11. Ebbinghaus, H. *Uber das Gedachtnis: Untersuchungen zur experimentellen Psychologie* (Dunker and Humbolt, Leipzig), transl. Ruger, H. A. and Byssenine, C. E. as *Memory: A Contribution to Experimental Psychology* (Dover, New York, 1913).

12. By way of contrast, Ebbinghaus's contemporary, Wundt, wrote a total of 53,735 pages – the equivalent of more than a 500-page book every year for a hundred years. George Miller, the Harvard psychologist, once commented: 'The sheer bulk of his writing made Wundt almost immune to criticism. A critic would be outwritten, evaded by qualifications, and buried under mountains of detail.' Quoted in Wilson, J. L., and the editors of *Life*. *The Mind* (Time, New York, 1964).

13. In reality, the experiments are more difficult than was thought by Ebbinghaus. Any psychologist who has used syllables in the laboratory knows perfectly well that they are not really nonsense – they set up a mass of associations that do vary in meaningfulness, possibly even more so than those aroused by common language with its conventional meaning. The 1930s brought a revolt against the Ebbinghaus school when the Cambridge psychologist Sir Frederic Bartlett discarded the use of nonsense syllables and began to study meaningful memory. He was mostly concerned that the experimental conditions should be as natural as possible. Bartlett challenged many artificial memory metaphors by arguing that memory is an active reconstruction of, rather than a passive store for, things past, and this reconstruction is in important ways a social act. Bartlett, F. C. *Remembering* (Cambridge University Press, 1932).

14. For studies of interference, primacy and recency *see* Baddeley, A. D. *Human Memory: Theory and Practice* (Allyn & Bacon, Boston, 1990); Baddeley, A. D., and Hitch, G. Recency Re-examined. In S. Dornic (ed.) *Attention and Performance* pp. 647–667 (Erlbaum, Hillsdale, 1997); Finger, S. *Origins of*

Neuroscience. A History of Explorations into Brain Function (Oxford University Press, 1994).

15. Müller, G. E., and Pilzecker, A. Experimentelle Beitrage zur Lehre vom Gedachtnis. *Zeitschrift fur Psychologie* (1890) 1, 1–300.

16. Throughout this book I discuss numerous animal experiments, some of which appear to be distinctly nasty. Although such experiments are always done under authorization of stringent laws and strict guidance, it is never easy or pleasant to experiment on animals. Memory research is aimed at understanding the basic brain mechanisms involved in learning and memory. If we, and by 'we' I mean us as people, us as society, want to have this knowledge, and to develop treatments to help millions of people suffering from memory disorders, there is no other way of doing this than to work on animals.

17. René Descartes's philosophy was a bold attempt to reconcile a mechanistic view of the material world with faith in God. Descartes's complete division between mind and body – 'I think, therefore I am' – has clouded western scientific and philosophical thinking for more than three centuries. This statement illustrates the opposite of what most biologists believe now about the relation between mind and body. As the neurologist Antonio Damasio writes in his book, *Descartes' Error* (Putnam, New York, 1994), 'We are, and then we think, and we think only in as much as we are, since thinking is indeed caused by the structures and operations of being.' Descartes' naive versions of memory models became essentials of modern memory concepts: representations subserved by physical traces in the brain, and experience-dependent facilitation of connections in these traces (*see* Chapter 6).

18. Darwin, C. *The Descent of Man and Selection in Relation to Sex* (Murray, London, 1871; reprinted 1981, Princeton University Press).

Chapter 2

1. James, W. *Principles of Psychology* pp. 646–648 (Holt, New York, 1890).

2. Aristophanes, quoted in Herrmann, D. J., and Chaffin, R. *Memory in Historical Perspective: The Literature Before Ebbinghaus* (Springer, New York, 1988).

3. Schacter, D. L., and Tulving, E. *Memory Systems 1994* (MIT Press, Cambridge, 1994).

4. For a general discussion on memory span procedures *see* Baddeley, A. D. *Human Memory: Theory and Practice* (Allyn & Bacon, Boston, 1990).

5. Miller, G. A. The magic number seven, plus or minus two. *Psychology Review* (1956) 9, 81–97. For chunking, *see also* Egan, D. E., and Schwartz, B. J. Chunking in recall of symbolic drawings. *Memory and Cognition* (1979) 7, 149–158.

6. Hunter, I. M. L. An exceptional memory. *British Journal of Psychology* (1977) 68, 155–164.

7. Ericsson, K. A., Chase, W. G., and Faloon, S. F. Acquisition of a memory skill. *Science* (1980) 208, 1181–1182.

8. Brown, J. Some tests of the decay theory of immediate memory. *Quarterly Journal of Experimental Psychology* (1958) 10, 12–21; Peterson, L. R., and Peterson, M. J. Short-term retention of individual verbal items. *Journal of Experimental Psychology* (1959) 58, 193–198.

9. Keppel, G., and Underwood, B. J. Proactive inhibition in short-term retention of single items. *Journal of Verbal Learning and Bahavior* (1962) 1, 153–161.

10. Schweickert, R., and Boruff, B. Short-term memory capacity: magic number or magic spell? *Journal of Experimental Psychology: Learning, Memory, and Cognition* (1986) 12, 419–425.

11. For historical analysis of the consolidation idea *see* Squire, L. R. *Memory and Brain* (Oxford University Press, New York, 1987); Polster, M. R., Nadel, L., and Schacter, D. L. Cognitive neuroscience analysis of memory: a historical perspective. *Journal of Cognitive Neuroscience* (1991) 3, 95–116; Lechner, H. A., Squire, L. R., and Byrne, J. H. 100 years of consolidation – remembering Müller and Pilzecker. *Learning and Memory* (1999), 77–87.

12. The terms 'retrograde' and 'anterograde' amnesia were coined by

French physician Charles Azam who in the late nineteenth century described memory loss in a patient with multiple personality. *See* Hacking, I. *Rewriting the Soul: Multiple Personality and the Sciences of Memory* (Princeton University Press, 1995).

13. Russell, W. R. *Brain, Memory, Learning* (Oxford, 1959).

14. For a description of N.A.'s case *see* Squire, L. R. *Memory and Brain* (Oxford University Press, New York, 1987).

15. K.F.'s case is described by Tulving, E. Remembering and knowing the past. *American Scientist* (1989) 77, 361–367.

16. Quoted in Rupp, R. *Committed to Memory* (Crown, New York, 1997).

17. Tulving, E. Episodic and semantic memory. In Tulving, E. and Donaldson, W. (eds) *Organization of Memory*, pp. 381–403 (Academic Press, New York, 1972); Tulving, E. *Elements of Episodic Memory* (Clarendon Press, Oxford, 1983); Remembering and knowing the past. *American Scientist* (1989) 77, 361–367.

18. Quoted in Rupp, R. *Committed to Memory* (Crown, New York, 1997).

19. Smith, E. E., Shoben, E. J., and Rips, L. J. Structure and process in semantic memory: a feature model for semantic decisions. *Psychological Review* (1974) 81, 214–241.

20. Collins, A. M., and Quillian, M. R. Retrieval time from semantic memory. *Journal of Verbal Learning and Verbal Behavior* (1969) 8, 240–247.

21. Collins, A. M., and Loftus, E. F. A spreading activation theory of semantic memory. *Psychological Review* (1975) 82, 407–428.

22. De Renzi, E., Liotti, M., and Nichelli, P. Semantic amnesia with preservation of autobiographic memory. A case report. *Cortex* (1987) 23, 575–597.

23. Warrington, E. K., and Shallice, T. Category specific semantic impairments. *Brain* (1984) 107, 829–854.

24. Frederick's case is reported in Schacter, D. L. *Searching for Memory* (Basic Books, 1996).

25. Cohen, N. J., and Squire, L. R. Preserved learning and retention of pattern analysing skill in amnesia: dissociation of knowing

how and knowing that. *Science* (1980) 210, 207–209. For general discussions on memory systems *see* Schacter, D. L., and Tulving, E. *Memory Systems 1994* (MIT Press, Cambridge, 1994); Eichenbaum, H. Declarative memory: insights from cognitive neurobiology. *Annual Review of Psychology* (1997) 48, 547–572; Squire, L. R. Memory systems. *C R Acad Sci* (1998) 321 (2–3): 153–156.

26. Warrington, E. K., and Weiskrantz, L. New method of testing long-term retention with special reference to amnesic patients. *Nature* (1968) 217, 972–974; Warrington, E. K., and Weiskrantz, L. Amnesic syndrome: consolidation or retrieval? *Nature* (1970) 228, 628–630; *see also* Weiskrantz, L. On issues and theories of the human amnesic syndrome. In Weinberger, N. M., McGaugh, J. L. and Lynch, G. (eds) *Memory Systems of the Brain*, pp. 380–415 (Guilford, New York, 1985).

27. For discussion of studies on priming *see* Schacter, D. L. *Searching for Memory* (Basic Books, New York, 1996); Tulving, E., and Schacter, D. L. Priming and human memory systems. *Science* (1990) 247, 301–306.

28. Dunn, R. Case of suspension of the mental faculties. *Lancet* (1845) ii, 588–590; Bergson, H. *Matter and Memory*, transl. N. Paul, M. and Palmer, W. S. (Swan Sonnenschein, London, 1911); Claparede, E. Recognition and me-ness. in *Organization and Pathology of Thought* pp. 58–75 (Columbia University Press, New York, 1951).

29. Graf, P., and Schacter, D. L. Implicit and explicit memory for new associations in normal subjects and amnesic patients. *Journal of Experimental Psychology: Learning, Memory, and Cognition* (1985) 11, 501–518.

30. Quoted in Rupp, R. *Committed to Memory* (Crown, New York, 1997).

31. For accounts of the localization debate *see* Marshall, J. The new organology. *Behavioural and Brain Sciences* (1980) 3, 23–25; Sizer, N. *Forty years in Phrenology: Embracing Recollections of History, Anecdote and Experience* (Fowler & Wells, New York, 1882); Gross, C. *Brain, Vision, Memory. Tales in the History of Neuroscience* (MIT Press, Cambridge 1998).

32. Broca, P. Sur la faculté du langage articulé. *Bulletin Sociology Antrhopology* (Paris 1865) 6, 337–393.

33. Wernicke, C. *Der aphasische Symptomencomplex* (Cohn und Weigert, Breslau, 1874); For details on the neuroanatomy of language *see* Damasio, A., and Damasio, H. Brain and language. *Scientific American* (1992) 267, 88–95.

34. For a review of Lashley's work *see* Breach, F., et al. (eds) *The Neuropsychology of Lashley. Selected Papers of K. S. Lashley* (McGraw-Hill, New York, 1960).

Chapter 3

1. For the original description of H.M.'s case *see* Scoville, W. B., and Milner, B. Loss of recent memory after bilateral hippocampal lesions. *Journal of Neurology, Neurosurgery and Psychiatry* (1957) 20, 11–21; For H.M.'s biography *see* Hilts, P. J. *Memory's Ghost: The Strange Tale of Mr. M and the Nature of Memory* (Simon & Schuster, New York, 1995).

2. Penfield, W. W. *The Mystery of the Mind* (Princeton University Press, 1975); For a recent review of Penfield's amnesic patients *see* Milner, B., Squire, L. R., and Kandel, E. R. Cognitive neuroscience and the study of memory. *Neuron* (1998) 20, 445–468.

3. Milner, B. S., Corkin, S., and Teuber, H. L. Further analysis of the hippocampal amnesic syndrome: 14 year follow up of H.M. *Neuropsychologia* (1968) 6, 215–234.

4. Gollin, E. S. Developmental studies of visual recognition of incomplete objects. *Perception Motor Skills* (1960) 11, 289–298.

5. Heindel, W. C., Salmon, D. P., Shults, C. W., Walicke, P. A., and Butters, N. Neuropsychological evidence for multiple implicit memory systems: a comparison of Alzheimer's, Huntington's, and Parkinson's Disease Patients. *Journal of Neuroscience* (1989) 9, 582–587.

6. For a review *see* Mishkin, M., and Appenzeller, T. The anatomy of memory. *Scientific American* (1987) June, 80–89; For an original report *see* Mishkin, M. Memory in monkeys severely impaired by combined but not separate removal of amygdala and hippocampus. *Nature* (1978) 273, 297–298.

7. Ibid. pp. 297–298.

8. Zola-Morgan, S., Squire, L. R. and Amaral, D. G. Human amnesia and the medial temporal region: enduring memory impairment following a bilateral lesion limited to field CA1 of the hippocampus. *Journal of Neuroscience* (1986) 6, 2950–2967; Zola-Morgan, S. Memory: clinical and anatomical aspects. In Feinberg, T. E. and Farah, M. (eds) *Behavioral Neurology and Neuropsychology* (McGraw-Hill, New York, 1996).

9. Reviewed by Squire, L. R. Memory and hippocampus: a synthesis from findings with rats, monkeys, and humans. *Psychological Review* (1992) 99, 195–231.

10. For a review, *see* Milner, B., Squire, L. R. and Kandel, E. R. Cognitive neuroscience and the study of memory. *Neuron* (1998) 20, 445–468.

11. For accounts of face and object recognition *see* De Haan, E., and Newcombe, F. What makes faces familiar? *New Scientist* (1991) February, 49–52; Sacks, O. *The Man Who Mistook His Wife for a Hat* (Summit Books, New York, 1985).

12. Ibid. pp. 49–52.

13. Ibid. pp. 49–52.

14. For experimental observations concerning Boswell *see* Damasio, A. R., Tranel, D., and Damasio, H. Amnesia caused by herpes simplex encephalitis, infarctions in basal forebrain, Alzheimer's disease and anoxia/ischemia. In Boller, F. and Grafman, J. (eds) *Handbook of Neuropsychology*, vol. 3, pp. 149–165 (Elsevier, Amsterdam, 1989); Damasio, A. R., Tranel, D., and Damasio, H. Face agnosia and the neural substrates of memory. *Annual Review of Neuroscience* (1990) 13, 89–109.

15. Reed, J. M., and Squire, L. R. Retrograde amnesia for facts and events: findings from four new cases. *Journal of Neuroscience* (1998) 3943–3954.

16. For this study and similar examples *see* Searleman, A., and Herrmann, D. *Memory from a Broader Perspective* (McGraw-Hill, New York, 1994).

17. Standing, L. Learning ten thousand pictures. *Quarterly Journal of Experimental Psychology* (1973) 25, 207–222.

18. Burke, D., MacKay, D. G., Worthley, J. S., and Wade, E. On the

tip of the tongue: what causes word finding failures in young and older adults? *Journal of Memory and Language* (1991) 30, 237–246.

19. Brown, R., and McNeill, D. The tip-of-the-tongue phenomenon. *Journal of Verbal Learning and Verbal Behavior* (1966) 5, 325–337; Brown, A. S. A review of the tip-of-the-tongue experience. *Psychological Bulletin* (1991) 109, 204–223.

20. Levelt, W. J., and Wheeldon, L. Do speakers have access to a mental syllabary? *Cognition* (1994) 50, 239–269.

21. For experiments on how the brain sorts and encodes names *see* Burton, M. Good morning, Mr … er. *New Scientist* (1994), 1 February, 39–41; Rees, A. If only I could remember her name. *New Scientist* (1994), December, 72–73; Burton, M., Noll, D. C., and Small, S. L. The anatomy of auditory word processing: individual variability. *Brain and Language* (1994), 77, 1, 119–131.

22. Damasio, A., and Damasio, H. Brain and language. *Scientific American* (1992) 267, 88–95.

23. For various accounts of spatial memory *see* O'Keefe, J., and Nadel, L. *The Hippocampus as a Cognitive Map* (Oxford University Press, 1978). For reviews of place cells and spatial memory *see* Muller, R. A quarter of a century of place cells. *Neuron* (1996) 17, 813–822; O'Keefe, J. Do hippocampal pyramidal cells signal non-spatial as well as spatial information? *Hippocampus* (1999) 9, 352–364; Burgess, N., Jackson, A., Hartley, T., and O'Keefe, J. Predictions derived from modelling the hippocampal role in navigation. *Biological Cybernetics* (2000) 83, 301–312.

24. Quoted in O'Keefe, J., and Nadel, L. *The Hippocampus as a Cognitive Map* (Oxford University Press, 1978).

25. Baddeley, A. D. *Working Memory* (Clarendon Press, Oxford, 1986). *See also* Goldman-Pakic, P. S. Working memory and the mind. *Scientific American* (1992) September, 111–117.

Chapter 4

1. Quoted in Halbfinger, D. Where fear lingers: a Special Report. A neighborhood gives peace a wary look *New York Times* (18 May, 1998).

2. Ibid. 18 May 1998.

3. Darwin, C. *The Expression of the Emotions in Man and Animals* (1872, reprinted by the University of Chicago Press, 1965).

4. Bekhterev, V. *Obshie Osnovi Refleksology Cheloveka* (in Russian), p. 175 (Gos. Izd. Moskva, Petrograd, 1923).

5. Long before Bekhterev's discovery, the Greek physician Hippocrates described an unusual case. When Nicanor began to drink, the sound of the flute, even the first note, would disturb him. Amazingly, he could listen to the flute during the day; only at nights, and only when he started to drink, would the terror of the flute descend upon him.

6. Pavlov, I. P., *Conditioned reflexes: An Investigation of the Physiological Activity of the Cerebral Cortex* (Oxford University Press, 1927).

7. The critical distinction between a common fear and a phobia is the degree to which it interferes with everyday life. For example, fear of snakes is not likely to interfere with everyday life and therefore is rarely considered a phobia. On the other hand, a fear of heights, if accompanied by avoidance of offices on the top floors of high buildings, of high-rise apartments and hotels or of rooftop restaurants, will interfere with work or leisure activities and is considered a phobia.

8. Beck, A. T., and Emery, G. *Anxiety Disorders and Phobias: A Cognitive Perspective* (Basic Books, New York, 1985).

9. Ohman, A. Fear and anxiety as emotional phenomena: clinical, phenomenological, evolutionary perspectives, and information-processing mechanisms. In Lewis, M. and Haviland, J. M. (eds) *Handbook of the Emotions*, pp. 511–536 (Guilford, New York, 1992).

10. For reviews of research on fear responses *see* LeDoux, J. E. Emotion, Memory, and the Brain. *Scientific American* (1994)

June, 50–57; Archer, J. Behavioral aspects of fear. In Sluckin, W.
(ed.) *Fear in Animals and Man* (Van Nostrand Reinhold, New
York, 1979); LeDoux, J. *The Emotional Brain* (Simon &
Schuster, New York, 1996); Davis, M. Neurobiology of fear
responses: the role of the amygdala. *Journal of Neuropsychiatry
and Clinical Neurosciences* (1997), 9, 382–402; Buchel, C.,
Morris, J., Dolan, R., and Friston, K. J. Brain systems mediating
aversive conditioning: an event-related fMRI study. *Neuron*
(1998) 20, 947–957.

11. Klüver, H., and Bucy, P. C. 'Psychic blindness' and other
symptoms following bilateral temporal lobectomy in rhesus
monkeys. *American Journal of Physiology* (1998) 119, 352–353;
Weiskrantz, L. Behavioral changes associated with ablation of
the amygdaloid complex in monkeys. *Journal of Comparative
Physiological Psychology* (1956) 49, 381–191. For more accounts
on the role of the amygdala in emotion *see* Aggleton, J. P. *The
Amygdala: Neurobiological Aspects of Emotion, Memory, and
Mental Dysfunction* (Wiley-Liss, New York, 1992).

12. The case of the man with no feelings is described in Goleman, D.
Emotional Intelligence (Bantam Books, New York, 1995). For
more accounts about feelings in people who lack an amygdala
see Ekman, P., and Davidson, R. *Questions About Emotion*
(Oxford University Press, New York, 1994).

13. Adolphs, R., Tranel, D., Damasio, H., and Damasio, A. Fear and
the human amygdala. *The Journal of Neuroscience* (1995) 15, 9,
5879–5891. For recent experiments on facial expressions and the
amygdala *see* Morris, J. S., Ohman, A., and Dolan, R. J.
Conscious and unconcious emotional learning in the human
amygdala. *Nature* (1998) 393, 467–470.

14. Scott, S. K., Young, A. W., Calder, A. J., Hellawell, D. J.,
Aggleton, J. P., and Johnson, M. Impaired auditory recognition of
fear and anger following bilateral amygdala lesions. *Nature*
(1998) 385, 254–257.

15. Bechara, A., Tranel, D., Damasio, H., Adolphs, R., Rockland, C.,
and Damasio, A. R. Double dissociation of conditioning and
declarative knowledge relative to the amygdala and
hippocampus in humans. *Science* (1995) 269, 1115–1118.

16. For the modulatory role of the amygdala in emotional memory *see* McGaugh, J. L., and Gold, P. E. Modulation of memory by electrical stimulation of the brain. In Rosenzweig, M. R. and Bennett, E. L. (eds) *Neural Mechanisms of Learning and Memory*, pp. 549–560 (MIT Press, 1976); Gold, P. E. Sweet Memories. *American Scientist* (1987) 75, 151–155; McGaugh, J. L. Neuromodulation and the storage of information: involvement of the amygdaloid complex. In Lister, R. G. and Weingartner, H. J. (eds) *Perspectives on Cognitive Neuroscience* pp. 279–299 (Oxford University Press, New York, 1991).

17. Cahill, L., Prins, B., Weber, M. and McGaugh, J. L. Beta-adrenergic activation and memory for emotional events. *Nature* (1994) 371, 702–704.

18. I should like to draw your attention to what I mean by 'emotion' and 'mood'. The root of the word 'emotion' is *emovere*, the Latin verb 'to move out', suggesting that emotions lead to actions. Emotion is a complex response involving physiological changes as a preparation for action, as well as changes in facial expression and often in body posture. Mood is a state of mind that is affected by the trend of our thoughts. We might be in a bad mood because of some sad thoughts but we do not necessarily take action.

19. For more information on state-dependent memory and emotion *see* Bower, G. Mood and memory. *American Psychology* (1981) February, 129–148; Mandler, G. Memory, arousal and mood. In Christianson, S. A. (ed.) *Handbook of Emotion and Memory: Research and Theory* (Erlbaum, Hillsdale, 1992); Bower, G. H. and Mayer, J. D. Failure to replicate mood dependent retrieval. *Bulletin of the Psychonomic Society* (1985) 18, 39–42; Ellis, H. C., and Ashbrook, P. W. The state of mood and memory research: a selective review. In Kuiken, D. (ed.) *Mood and Memory: Theory, Resarch, and Applications* (special issue). *Journal of Social Behavior and Personality* (1989) 4, 1–21.

20. Some researchers have now questioned the reliability of mood-dependent memory. There is now more evidence for 'mood congruence', which occurs when a person's current mood causes selective encoding and retrieval of material that is consistent (congruent) with the prevailing mood state.

21. Brown, R., and Kulik, J. Flashbulb memories. *Cognition* (1977) 5, 73–99.

22. Neisser, U., and Harsch, N. Phantom flashbulbs: false recollections of hearing the news about Challenger. In Winograd, E. and Neisser, U. (eds) *Affect and Accuracy in Recall: Studies of Flashbulb Memories* pp. 9–31 (Cambrige University Press, New York, 1992). For general information about flashbulb memories and remembering in natural context *see* Neisser, U. *Memory Observed* (Freeman, New York, 1982).

23. Conway, M. A. *Flashbulb Memories* (Erlbaum, Hillsdale, 1995).

24. Larsen, S. F. Potential flashbulbs: memories of ordinary news as baseline. In Winograd, E. and Neisser, U. (eds) *Affect and Accuracy in Recall: Studies of 'Flashbulb Memories'* pp. 32–64 (Cambridge University Press, New York, 1992).

25. James, W. *Principles of Psychology* (Holt, New York, 1992).

26. During the 1980s and 1990s there was an explosion of reports (mainly in the USA) in which people, especially young women undergoing psychotherapy, seemingly remembered childhood sexual abuse, torture or even satanic cults, that they had repressed for years. While not denying that it is possible to recover traumatic memories much later in life, many researchers and medical doctors are critical of such 'recovered' memories (called 'false memory' syndrome). In 1994, the American Psychiatric Association cautioned against false memories and expressed scepticism about using hypnosis and other suggestive techniques to help elicit them. A growing number of patients across America have won lawsuits that accused therapists of leading them to recount false memories. In November 1997, in Houston, a grand jury brought the first criminal charges in cases involving accusations that therapists invoked false memories. The formal charges were that a hospital administrator and four therapists had collected millions of dollars in fraudulent insurance payments by exaggerating patients' diagnoses and convincing them that they had been part of a satanic cult (reported in Belluck, P. Woman Wins Suit Claiming Therapists Invoked Traumatic Memories. *New York Times* [6 November, 1997]). For general discussions on false

memory syndrome *see* Schacter, D. L. Memory wars. *Scientific American* (1995) April, 135–139; Holmes, B. When memory plays us false. *New Scientist* (1994) 23, 32–35.

27. Janet, P. *Psychological Healing*, vol. 1, pp. 661–66, transl. Paul, E. and Paul, C. (1925, reprinted by Macmillan, 1991).

28. Freud, S. *Beyond the Pleasure Principle*. Standard Edition, vol. 18, pp. 7–64 (Hogarth Press, London, 1955).

29. Lessing, D. *A Small Personal Voice* p. 87 (Random House, New York, 1975).

30. Wilkinson, C. B. Aftermath of a disaster: the collapse of the Hyatt Regency Hotel skywalks. *American Journal of Psychiatry* (1983) 140, 1134–1139.

31. For discussions of traumatic disorders *see* Herman, J. L. *Trauma and Recovery* (Basic Books, New York, 1992).

32. Lifton, R. J. The concept of the survivor. In Dimsdale, J. E. (ed.) *Survivors, Victims, and Perpetrators: Essays on the Nazi Holocaust* pp. 113–126 (Hemisphere, New York, 1980).

33. O'Brien, T. How to tell a true war story. In *The Things They Carried* p. 89 (Houghton Mifflin, Boston, 1990). Quoted in Herman, J. L. *Trauma and Recovery*, p. 38 (Basic Books, New York, 1992).

34. Quotes are from Langer, L. *Holocaust Testimonies: The Ruins of Memory* (Yale University Press, 1991).

35. Quote is from Schemo, D. J. In Woods of Georgia Echoes of Balkan Terror. *New York Times* (16 June, 1999).

36. For examples of traumatic memories in children *see* Terr, L. What happens to early memories of trauma? A study of twenty children under age five at the time of documented traumatic events. *Journal of the American Academy of Child and Adolescent Psychiatry* (1988) 27, 96–104; Terr, L. *Too Scared to Cry* (HarperCollins, New York, 1990); Terr, L. *Unchained Memories* (Basic Books, New York, 1994).

37. Schachter, D., *Searching for Memory* (Basic Books, New York, 1996).

Chapter 5

1. Quote is from Luria, A. R. *The Mind of a Mnemonist* (Basic Books, New York, 1968).
2. Ibid.
3. People with synaesthesia are described by Cytowic, R. E. *Synesthesia: A union of the Senses* (Springer, New York, 1989); Cytowic, R. E. *The Man Who Tasted Shapes* (Warner Books, New York, 1993); Motluk, A. The sweet smell of purple. *New Scientist* (1994) 13 August, 33–37.
4. Nabokov, V. *Speak, memory: An Autobiography Revisited* (Putman, New York, 1966).
5. Luria, A. R. (1968) op. cit.
6. The case of Elizabeth was reported by Stromeyer, C. F. Eidetikers. *Psychology Today* (1970) 76–80.
7. Haber, R. N. Twenty years hunting eidetic imagery: where's the ghost? *The Behavioural and Brain Sciences* (1979) 2, 583–594; Haber, R. N., and Haber, L. R. The characteristics of eidetic imagery. In Obler, L. K. and Fein, D. (eds) *The Exceptional Brain: Neuropsychology of Talent and Special Abilities* pp. 218–241 (Guilford Press, New York, 1988).
8. For fascinating accounts of people with exceptional memories, *see* Neisser, U. *Memory Observed* (Freeman, New York, 1982).

Chapter 6

1. Ramon y Cajal, S. The structure and connections of neurons. In *Nobel Lectures: Physiology or Medicine* (1901–1921) pp. 220–253 (Elsevier, Amsterdam, 1967).
2. For detailed accounts of cell biology of the neuron *see* Kandel, E. R., Schwartz, J. H., and Jessell, T. M. *Principles of Neural Science* (Elsevier, Amsterdam, 1999).
3. Meckler, I. B. Mechanism of biological memory. *Nature* (1967) 215, 481–484.
4. Conrad, M. Molecular information structures in the brain. *Journal of Neuroscience Research* (1974) 2, 233–54.
5. Friedrich, P. Protein structure: the primary substrate of memory. *Neuroscience* (1990) 35, 1–7.

6. Memory transfer experiments are described by McConnell, J. V. Memory transfer through cannibalism in planarians. *Journal of Neuropsychiatry* (1962) 3 (suppl. 2) 42–48; Babich, F. R., Jacobson, A. L., Bubash, S., and Jacobson, A. Transfer of a response to naive rats by injection of ribonucleic acid extracted from trained rats. *Science* (1965) 149, 656–657; Ungar, G., Desiderio, D. M., and Parr, W. Isolation, identification and synthesis of a specific behaviour-inducing brain peptide. *Nature* (1972) 238, 198–202; Stewart, W. W. Comments on the chemistry of scotophobin. *Nature* (1972) 238, 202–209; For criticism, *see* Corning, W. C., and Riccio, D. The planarian controversy. In Byrne, W. L. (ed.) *Molecular Approaches to Learning and Memory* pp. 107–50 (Academic Press, New York, 1970); Byrne, W. L., and 22 others. Memory transfer. *Science* (1966) 153, 658–659.

7. Rose, S. *The Making of Memory* (Bantam Books, New York, 1992).

8. Sherrington, C. S. The central nervous system. In *A Textbook of Physiology*, 7th ed vol. 3, Foster, M. (ed.), (Macmillan, London, 1897).

9. Quoted in Rosenzweig, M. R. Aspects of the search for neural mechanisms of memory. *Annual Review of Psychology* (1996) 47, 33–57.

10. Ramon y Cajal, S. The Croonian Lecture: La fine structure des centres nerveux. *Proceedings of the Royal Society* (1894) B 55, 444–467.

11. Milner, P. M. The mind and Donald O. Hebb. *Scientific American* (1993) January, 124–129.

12. Hebb, D. O. *The Organization of Behaviour* (Wiley, New York, 1949).

13. Rosenzweig, M. R., Bennett, E. L., and Diamond, M. C. Effects of differential environments on brain anatomy and brain chemistry. In Zubin, J. and Jervis, G. (eds) *Psychopathology of Mental Development* pp. 45–56 (Grune & Stratton, New York, 1967); Rosenzweig, M. R. Experience, memory, and the brain. *American Psychologist* (1984) 39, 365–376.

14. Wiesel, T. N., and Hubel, D. H. Comparison of the effects of unilateral and bilateral eye closure on cortical unit responses in kittens. *Journal of Neurophysiology* (1965) 28, 1029–1040; Hubel, D. H., and Wiesel, T. N. Brain mechanisms of vision. *Scientific American* (1979) 241, 150–163.

15. Nottebohm, F. Brain pathways for vocal learning in birds: a review of the first ten years. *Progress in Psychobiology and Physiological Psychology* (1980) 9, 85–124.

16. Stewart, M. G. Morphological correlates of long-term memory in the chick forebrain consequent on passive avoidance learning. In Squire, L. R. and Lindenlaub, E. (eds) *The Biology of Memory*, pp. 193–215 (Schattauer, (1990); Horn, G., Bateson, P. P. G., and Rose, S. P. R. Experience and plasticity in the nervous system. *Science* (1973) 181, 506–514. For general accounts on memory and plasticity research in chicks *see* Rose, S. *The Making of Memory* (Bantam Books, New York, 1992).

17. Kempermann, G., Kuhn, H. G., and Gage, F. H. More hippocampal neurons in adult mice living in an enriched environment. *Nature* (1997) 386, 493–495.

18. For reviews *see* Kandel, E. R., and Hawkins, R. D. The biological basis of learning and individuality. *Scientific American* (1992) September, 79–86; Bailey, C. H., and Kandel, E. R. Structural changes accompanying memory storage. *Annual Review of Psychology* (1993) 55, 397–426.

19. Quoted in Rosenzweig, M. R. Aspects of the search for neural mechanisms of memory. *Annual Review of Psychology* (1996) 47, 33–57.

20. For general accounts of research on *Aplysia see* Kandel, E. R. Small systems of neurons. *Scientific American* (1979) 241, 66–76; Squire, L. and Kandel, E. R. *Memory* (Freeman, New York, 1999).

21. Kandel, trained as a psychiatrist, was first exposed to *Aplysia* research in Ladislav Tauc's laboratory, in Paris in the 1960s. He spent six scientifically productive months working on short-term processes such as habituation. But Angelique Arvanitaki was probably the first to realize the experimental advantage that *Aplysia* offers in the study of its neural networks.

22. Pribram, K. *Languages of the Brain* (Prentice-Hall, New York, 1971).

23. The studies of the gill-withdrawal reflex are a classic example of research using reductive and simplifying steps. More detailed accounts of this are given in Yadin Dudai's *The Neurobiology of Memory* and Steven Rose's *The Making of Memory*.

24. Bliss, T. V. P., and Lomo, T. Long-lasting potentiation of synaptic transmission in the dentate area of the anaesthetised rabbit following stimulation of the perforant path. *Journal of Physiology* (1973) 232, 331–356.

25. For reviews of LTP research *see* Churchland, P. S., and Sejnowski, T. J. *The Computational Brain* (MIT Press, 1992); Bliss, T. V. P., and Collingridge, G. L. A synaptic model of memory: long-term potentiation in the hippocampus. *Nature* (1993) 232, 31–39; Albright, T. D., Jessell, T. M., Kandel, E. R., and Posner, M. I. Neural science: a century of progress and the mysteries that remain. *Cell* review supplement to vol. 100, *Neuron* (2000) 25, S1–S55.

26. For reviews *see* Morris, R. G. M., Davis, S. and Butcher, S. P. Hippocampal synaptic plasticity and NMDA receptors: a role in information storage? *Philosophical Transactions of the Royal Society of London* (1990) B 329, 187–204; Barnes, C. A., Erickson, C. A., Davis, S., and McNaughton, B. L. Hippocampal synaptic enhancement as a basis for learning and memory: a selected review of current evidence from behaving animals. In McGaugh, J. L., Weinberger, N. M., and Lynch, G. (eds) *Brain and Memory: Modulation and Mediation of neuroplasticity*, pp. 259–276 (Oxford University Press, New York, 1995).

27. Rogan, M. T., Staubli, U. V., and LeDoux, J. E., Fear conditioning induces associative long-term potentiation in the amygdala. *Nature* (1997) 390 (6660), 604–607. For a review of LTP and the amygdala *see* Fanselow, M. S., and LeDoux, J. E. Why we think plasticity underlying Pavlovian fear conditioning occurs in the basolateral amygdala. *Neuron* (1999) 23, 2, 229–32.

Chapter 7

1. Silva, A. J., Stevens, C. F., Tonegawa, S., Wang, Y. Deficient
   hippocampal long-term potentiation in alpha-calcium-
   calmodulin kinase II mutant mice. *Science* (1992) 257 (5067),
   201–206; Silva, A. J., Paylor, R., Wehner, J. M., and Tonegawa, S.
   Impaired spatial learning in alpha-calcium-calmodulin kinase II
   mutant mice. *Science* (1992) 257 (5067), 206–11.
2. This building is famous for its Hazen Tower that bears a plaque
   inscribed with the initials of the four chemical letters that make
   up the backbone of the DNA molecule: cytosine, guanine,
   adenine, and thymine. The bell inside rings every hour and
   sounds like a deep 'G' tone.
3. Capecci, M. The new mouse genetics: altering the genome by
   gene targeting. *Trends in Genetics* (1989) 5, 3, 70–76.
4. Historically, the origin of genetics, including behavioural
   genetics, traces its roots to the mouse. The fact that crossing a
   white mouse with a grey one produced only grey offspring in the
   first generation, and both greys and albinos subsequently, was
   described by Darwin in 1886, although the waltzing mouse,
   possibly the first behavioural mutant, was known from at least
   80 BC. During the late Graeco-Roman and early Christian era
   mice found their place in the history of medicine. However,
   until the early years of the seventeenth century, mice were not
   used in experimental studies. After the rediscovery of
   Mendelism in 1900, the mouse became the mammal of primary
   choice for geneticists. Laboratory mice became popular as
   subjects of behavioural genetics in the 1940s and they have been
   used since that time in neuropsychological studies in general.
   There are no precise figures for the annual use of mice in
   research, but estimates place the number for the United States
   at more than 20 million.
5. For reviews *see* Benzer, S. Genetic dissection of behavior.
   Scientific American (1973) 229, 24–37; Dudai, Y. Genetic
   dissection of learning and short term memory in Drosophila.
   Annual Review of Neuroscience (1988) 11, 537–63; Dubnau, J.
   and Tully, T. Gene discovery in *Drosophila*: new insights for

learning and memory. *Annual Review of Neuroscience* (1998) 21, 407–444.

6. For reviews *see* Grant, S. G. N., and Silva, A. J. Targeting learning. *Trends in Neurosciences* (1994) 17, 71–75.

7. Grant, S. G., O'Dell, T. J., Karl, K. A., Stein, P. L., Soriano, P., and Kandel, E. R. Impaired long-term potentiation, spatial learning, and hippocampal development in fyn mutant mice. *Science* (1992) 258 (5090), 1903–10.

8. Silva, A. J., Rosalh, T. W., Chapman, P. F, Marowitz, Z., Friedman, E., Frankland, P. W., Cioffi, D., Sudhof, T. C. and Bourtchouladze, R. A. Impaired learning in mice with abnormal short-lived plasticity. *Current Biology* (1996) 6, 11, 1509–1518.

9. Giese, K. P., Fedorov, N. B., Filipovski, R. K., and Silva, A. J. Autophosphorylation at Thr^{286} of the calcium-calmodulin kinase II in LTP and learning. *Science* (1998) 279, 870–873; Cho, Y. H., Giese, K. P., Tanila, H., Silva, A. J., and Eichenbaum, H. Abnormal hippocampal spatial representation in αCaMKII^{Thr286} and CREB mice. *Science* (1998) 279, 867–869.

10. Tsien, J. Z., Heurta, P. T., and Tonegawa, S. The essential role of hippocampal CA1 NMDA receptor-dependent synaptic plasticity in spatial memory. *Cell* (1996) 87, 1327–1338.

11. For review *see* Mayford, M., and Kandel, E. R. Genetic approaches to memory storage. *Trends in Genetics* (1999) 15, 463–470.

12. For review *see* Dubnau, J., and Tully, T. Gene discovery in *Drosophila*: new insights for learning and memory. *Annual Review of Neuroscience* (1998) 21, 407–444.

13. Dash, P. K., Hochner, B., and Kandel, E. R. Injection of the cAMP-responsive element into the nucleus of *Aplysia* sensory neurons blocks long-term facilitation. *Nature* (1990) 345, 718–721.

14. *Newsday*, 7 October 1994; *Wall Street Journal*, 27 February 1997.

15. Yin, J. C. P., Wallach, J. S., Del Vecchio, M., Wilder, E. L., Zhou, H., Quin, W. G., and Tully, T. Induction of a dominant negative CREB transgene specifically blocks long-term memory in Drosophila. *Cell* (1994) 79, 49–58.

16. Bourtchouladze, R., Frengeulli, B., Blendy, J., Cioffi, D., Schutz,

G., and Silva, A. J. Deficient long-term memory in mice with a targeted mutation of the cAMP-responsive element binding protein. *Cell* (1994) 79, 59–68.

17. For reviews *see* Frank, D. A., and Greenberg, M. E. CREB: a mediator of long-term memory from mollusks to mammals. *Cell* (1994) 79, 5–8; Mayford, M., Abel, T., and Kandel, E. R. Transgenic approaches to cognition. *Current Opinions in Neurobiology* (1995) 5, 141–148; Connolly, J. B., and Tully, T. You must remember this. *The Sciences* (1996) May/June, 37–42; Hall, S. Our memories, our selves. *New York Times Magazine* (1998) Feb. 15, 26–49; Albright, T. D., Jessell, T. M., Kandel, E. R., and Posner, M. I. Neural Science: a century of progress and the mysteries that remain. *Cell*, 2000 Review Supplement to vol. 100, *Neuron* 25, S1–S55.

18. Abel, T., Nguyen, P., Barad, M., Deuel, T., Kandel, E. R. and Bourtchouladze, R. A. Genetic demonstration of a role for PKA in the late phase of LTP and in hippocampus-based long-term memory. *Cell* (1997), 88, 615–626.

19. For comments *see* Tully, T. Regulation of gene expression and its role in long-term memory and synaptic plasticity. *Proceedings of the National Academy of Sciences* (1997) 94, 4239–4241. For original reports *see* Yin, J. C. P., Del Vecchio, M., Zhou, H., and Tully, T. CREB as a memory modulator: induced expression of a CREB2 activator isoform enhances long-term memory in Drosophila. *Cell* (1995) 81, 107–115; Bartsch, D., Ghirardy, M., Skehel, et al., CREB-2ATF-4 as a repressor of long-term facilitation in Aplasia: Relief of repression converts a transient facilitation into a long-term functional and structural change. *Cell* (1995) 83, 979–992; Kogan, J. H., Frankland, P. W., Blendy, J. A., Coblentz, J., Marowitz, Z., Schutz, G., and Silva, A. J. Spaced training induces normal long-term memory in CREB mutant mice. *Current Biology* (1996) 7, 1–11; Guzowski, J. F., and McGaugh, J. Antisense oligodeoxynucleotide-mediated disruption of hippocampal CREB protein levels impairs memory of a spatial task. *Proceedings of the National Academy of Sciences* (1997) 94, 2693–2698; Bernabeu, R., Beviluqua, P., Ardenghi, E., Bromberg, P., Schmitz, M., Bianchin, I., and

Medina, J. Involvement of hippocampal cAMP/cAMP-dependent protein kinase signaling pathways in a late memory consolidation phase of aversively motivated learning in rats. *Proceedings of the National Academy of Sciences* (1997) 94, 7041–7046.

20. Quoted in Hall, S. Our memories, our selves. *New York Times Magazine* (February 1998) 15, 26–49.

21. Borges, J. L., Funes the Memorious. In *Fictions* (Calder, London, 1965).

Index

Note: Page numbers *in italics* denote figures. Page numbers followed by n. and a number refer to a note on that page.